P9-CMS-537

# PRESENT WITH CONFIDENCE

## Fear No More!

**Written by Micki Holliday**
**Edited by National Press Publications**

## NATIONAL PRESS PUBLICATIONS

*A Division of Rockhurst University Continuing Education Center, Inc.*
6901 West 63rd Street • P.O. Box 2949 • Shawnee Mission, Kansas 66201-1349
1-800-258-7248 • 1-913-432-7755

National Press Publications endorses nonsexist language. In an effort to make this handbook clear, consistent and easy to read, we have used "he" throughout the odd-numbered chapters and "she" throughout the even-numbered chapters. The copy is not intended to be sexist.

***Present with Confidence — Fear No More!***

Published by National Press Publications, Inc.
Copyright 2000 by National Press Publications, Inc.
A Division of Rockhurst University Continuing Education Center, Inc.

Printed in the United States of America

 2  3  4  5  6  7  8  9  10

ISBN 1-55852-231-X

# Table of Contents

# INTRODUCTION

Do you know what Americans' number one fear is, according to survey after survey? It's not death or taxes, as you might expect. Believe it or not, Americans fear public speaking more than anything else.

Our palms sweat, our hands shake and our hearts race just at the very thought of getting up before an audience. We fear forgetting what we have to say, being embarrassed and ridiculed by others, being labeled as failures by bosses — all of which can damage our careers and reputations.

The keys to overcoming this fear are P & P — better known as preparation and practice. If you adequately prepare what you have to say and then practice how and when to say it, chances are slim that you'll forget, fail or be embarrassed.

The old adage:

> *"The room was hushed*
> *the speaker mute*
> *he'd left his notes in his other suit."*

will never apply to you.

After you have read this handbook, you should feel much more comfortable and confident about speaking to groups of people, no matter how large or how small. In fact, you'll probably be saying, "Let me at them!" All it takes are preparation, practice and some simple speaking techniques. Just keep in mind, the more you present, the easier it becomes and the better you get. Remember: P & P!

# 1 GETTING STARTED AS A PRESENTER

After reading this chapter you will know:

- how to analyze your audience to best meet its needs

- how to deal with a hostile audience

- how to keep your audience interested

Let's say your boss has just selected you to present the quarterly sales report to the entire staff next week. Or, maybe as a United Way volunteer, you have been asked to talk to local civic groups about how they can get involved in this year's fund-raising campaign. In either case, you've been called upon to speak — to get up in front of a group of colleagues or a room full of strangers.

Kind of a scary thought, isn't it? It doesn't have to be. You can learn how to present material confidently and competently, while making the most of your own personal speaking style.

## Presentation Facts

- **People like to hear and talk about themselves.** They're more likely to hear what you have to say if you talk about them. For instance, try complimenting your audience members. Tell them how refreshed and attentive they look, particularly if your presentation is first thing in the morning. Note something about the organization, the community or the city.

- **We "present" all the time.** Everyone, at one time or another, has to get up in front of people and talk. It may happen before a large group, such as a church congregation, or a small group, such as a book club you belong to. Whatever the situation, the key is knowing your material well enough to talk comfortably.

- **Good presenters control events and do the unexpected.** When you begin a presentation, your audience members always have "carryover tapes" — things already on their minds. Just because you're ready to speak doesn't mean they're ready to listen. "Carryover tapes" include distractions, such as the fight they had with their spouse that morning or the report they need to turn in the next day. People will be more inclined to shut down their tapes if you're creative and imaginative. Start with an "unexpected."

- **The bridge to a positive presentation is a positive start.** To get the audience's attention, you might try reciting a soliloquy or quote from Shakespeare, presenting a puzzle, or challenging with questions to hook interest. If you make a strong start, people are more likely to listen and keep listening throughout your presentation.

- **People will judge you and draw conclusions about you even before you open your mouth.** It's unfortunate, but it's typical human behavior. Control and plan your stance, your walk, your posture.

- **Focus on your dress, mood, tone and expertise.** These are the immediate things you can do something about, when it comes to how your audience perceives you. Choose dress that's appropriate for the occasion. It's always a good idea to dress the same as or slightly above your audience. Avoid something totally different unless you have to wear a costume or uniform. Keep your mood positive and your tone of voice pleasant. Let your expertise speak for itself.

No matter what stage you're at in your career, effective presentation skills will not only help you stay there — they'll help you get ahead as well. Develop your skills on an ongoing basis. Begin by realizing how much people appreciate the spoken word. As new high-tech communication methods become a way of life, people appreciate hearing someone speak with confidence and expertise.

Here are some tips that will develop solid skills which will aid you in your professional and personal life:

- **Become a fierce critic of speakers.** Every time you watch a presentation, look at everything the person says and does, the room setup and the visuals. Soon you'll pick up on many things you'll want to try — and many things you'll want to avoid. The more intensely you study presentations, the more you'll learn about them.

  Many books, tapes and seminars have been developed to help people with their presentation skills, but there is no exact science. A personal style is what sets you apart. By being a speaker's critic, you are constantly developing presentation skills.

- **Learn to enjoy anxiety.** This can happen easily if you realize that the most rewarding things in life come with some anxiety. Visualize how healthy you feel when you enjoy the emotions that anxiety creates — such as excitement or joy — and the payoff following the anxiety-causing event. By learning to enjoy the anxiety you experience before giving a presentation, you will develop habits to help you control and enjoy anxiety in other phases of your life.

- **Participate in group discussion whenever possible.** Here is something people can take advantage of regularly but often neglect to do. Consider it no-cost training. When you participate in workplace group discussion, you get used to hearing your voice and expressing your thoughts in a professional setting. When appropriate, stand up while you're talking.

- **Keep it simple** — both your message and its delivery. As you become a more advanced speaker, you can be as creative as you want. In the early stages of your speaking career, though, it's a good idea to keep it simple and stay on the topic. Develop at your own pace; don't try something too complex if you're not ready.

To summarize, three elements that are keys to your success are your:

1. Self-presentation

2. Connection

3. Positioning

Self-presentation includes verbal and nonverbal behaviors. It is viewed in how you stand, your posture, poise, walk, and eye contact. It is expressed in your manner of dress, overall image, voice, tone, and modality. It is captured in grammar and word choice. Critical are the overviews, summaries and transitions between topics. It is this competency that initiates your audiences' assessment of you. The immediate result of this competency is that your audience perceives you as knowledgeable, to be respected, a worthy role model.

Connection implies your rapport with your audience. It is your ability to connect with individuals, to talk *with* rather than *at* them. Done through stories, examples, previous experiences, questions, exercises, overheads that link information, and/or discussions with individuals, this skill personalizes your message. The result of this competency is that your audience feels you care about them.

Positioning is the skill by which you give relevancy and value to your message. The information is presented in such a way that your audience immediately sees the benefit of the specific information to them, their business or particular situation. Your information is presented in a manner that is cogent to the audience's personal and business needs. This competency results in their recognition of the value of what you say.

Think about how you might positively begin a presentation for each of the following occasions. In the space below, briefly explain how you would get off to a good start.

1. Your boss has asked you to give the quarterly sales report at the next staff meeting.

2. As a United Way volunteer, you've been asked to speak to a Rotary Club about the annual fund-raising campaign.

3. As the newly elected president of a service organization, you need to outline your goals for the coming year.

**The Five Elements of a** Reflections

# Presentation

Every good presentation has five important elements, which are shown in the following list. The first is its arrangement — how you put it together. This includes self-presentation. Next are the sources you rely upon, such as illustrations, examples, your own appeal as a speaker and even audience participation. These allow you to position information. The last three elements include your style, ability to remember what you have to say and your delivery. These cause your connection with your audience.

**ARRANGEMENT**

- Theme
- Introduction
  - Attention
  - Rapport
  - Orientation
- Outline
- Body
  - Unity
  - Movement
  - Transitions
- Conclusion
  - Arouse
  - Summarize
  - Apply

**SOURCES**

- Speaker's appeal as a person
- Audience involvement
- Logical flow to material
- Use of examples/illustrations

**STYLE**

- Clear
- Forceful
- Interesting
- Contrasts
- Imagination
- Variety

**MEMORY**

- Grasp
- Spontaneity

**DELIVERY**

- Attitude
- Directness
- Body language
- Voice
- Pronunciation

In 1884, John Milton Gregory published his landmark *Seven Laws of Teaching*, one of the clearest and most enduring statements on the art and skill of teaching. His points provide direction to the elements of presentation.

**1. Know the subject.**

- Study the material fresh each time.

- Seek out and use illustrations from real life.

- Use a natural order of truth, from the simple to the complex.

**2. Generate audience interest.**

Gain and keep the attention and interest of your audience.

- Use a variety of presentation techniques: visual aids, stories, illustrations, questions and discussion.

- Make your presentation interactive by asking questions.

**3. Use words that your audience knows.**

- Use short sentences.

- Explain new ideas by using objects, visual aids, slides, pictures, analogies and discussion.

**4. Build on known truths.**

Relate your points and illustrations to what your audience has experienced.

- Help your audience understand that practical new knowledge is usable in life experience.

5.  **Stimulate self-learning.**

    - Use practical exercises and illustrations that activate audience members' imaginations and get them involved.

    - Encourage your audience to try new skills and seek new knowledge. Demystify the unknown.

6.  **Learn by doing.**

    - Stimulate audience questioning, answering and participation.

    - Make sure your audience's actions are practical. An activity must lead somewhere and go there for a reason.

7.  **Tell them, tell them again, then tell them what you told them.**

    - Remember that review is the final touch to your presentation.

## Audience Analysis

Before you agree to give a presentation, you should know something about your audience. Why is this so important? Because the more you know about the people you'll be speaking to, the better you can meet their needs. And really, that's what public speaking is all about — meeting your audience's needs or providing them with information or ideas they can use.

One of the first things you'll want to know is the size of the group you're going to address. Audience size can be broken down into three basic groups:

1.  One to 10 people — an intimate group

2.  11 to 50 people — a small group

3.  51+ people — a large group

Knowing the size of the group will help you determine several things, such as how many handouts to prepare, how you'll interact with audience members, and whether you'll need a microphone to project your voice. For example, if you're using computer slides or an overhead, a 6-foot projection screen will work just fine for an intimate or small group. However, you'll need a much larger screen for an audience of 100 or more.

Similarly your dynamics, or interaction with the audience, should change, depending on audience size. With a bigger group, presenters tend to get lost in the crowd. Compensate by moving around more, maximizing eye contact with as many people as possible, and encouraging audience participation. If using a computer, have a remote control to move slides. Unfortunately, people can hide more easily in a crowd, so getting them involved is a challenge. Also, try to keep the length of your presentation reasonable. People tend to fidget and lose interest when speakers drag on, especially in large audiences.

Be sure you know who will be in the audience. In a work-related setting, it could be your superiors, peers, subordinates, or a combination of the three. In other cases, you may be talking to a special-interest group, such as a political organization or PTA. Whatever the audience makeup, you'll want to prepare your presentation a bit differently to meet its specific needs.

Here are a few tips for various audiences.

- **Superiors.** Never tell your superiors what to do. Instead, offer suggestions or recommendations. This is probably the most intimidating group to speak to, but the truth is these people want you to succeed. They want to show you off and brag about you. "I taught Bob here everything he knows." If your presentation goes well, then you look good and they look good. If it doesn't, then you look bad and so do they. They tend to take your speaking successes and failures personally.

- **Peers.** Unlike superiors, you usually can tell peers what they should do or what they should know. Occasionally, you'll run into a peer who thinks you have no business being a presenter. This person has the attitude, "I've been here longer," or "I have a higher degree," or "I've worked on this project longer." If you encounter a situation like this, share your beliefs or information instead of telling how it should be. Using a "Here it is ..." approach should diminish their attitude.

- **Subordinates.** This is the easiest audience to address by far. These people are accustomed to seeing you as a teacher, trainer, instructor or coach. They'll typically listen to what you have to say as long as you don't display a superior attitude.

- **Special-interest groups.** These are groups you might speak to in the community, away from work. In this setting, it's important to relate positive, persuasive experiences. For example, if you're a volunteer for the American Red Cross and you're trying to recruit blood donors, you might talk about how blood donations save lives. Better yet, you might ask someone whose life has been saved to come along with you. A testimonial is very persuasive because it plays on people's emotions and encourages them to take action.

## Understand Audience Members to Win Them Over

| Composition | Interests |
| --- | --- |
| Accountants | Latest software, recent changes in tax code |
| Computer specialists, Systems analysts | Correct information, properly used jargon |
| Educators | Homogeneous vs. class grouping, budget, tenure |
| Engineers | Solid information, professionally delivered, visual displays, relevant, well-prepared charts |
| Industry regulators | Can take offense at radical environmental ideas |
| Insurance brokers | Sales techniques, advertising methods, concerns of small-business owners |
| Lawyers | Avoid lawyer jokes |
| Librarians | No quips about eagle-eyed matrons with severe hairdos, use the title "Information Specialists," center on computer catalogs |
| Marketing personnel | What's in, what's out, ideas about vendors, trends |
| Medical workers | No doctor jokes to kick off speech, relationships, perceptions, laws, reform |
| Retail workers | Real estate costs, theft rates, popular trends |
| Self-employed | Medical coverage, retirement plans, child-care, computer hookups, networking |
| Small-business owners | Different focus than large department store owners, competition from malls, superstores |
| Stock and bond brokers | Volatile markets, wide-ranged interests |

## Dealing with Hostile Audiences

What kind of a reaction do you expect from your audience? Will it be receptive or hostile? When speaking, there are two kinds of hostilities: the kind that's waiting for you (built-in hostility) and the kind that develops. In both cases, you must acknowledge that the hostility exists.

Perhaps you're giving a presentation during a meeting and someone unexpectedly challenges you. You can stop and say, "What's happening here? We need to talk about this." An example of built-in hostility is having to tell your employees that their health care insurance premiums are about to double. The best advice is to deliver the information in a compassionate, straightforward manner. Don't try to sugarcoat the truth.

If you face hostilities like these when speaking, don't take them personally. In most cases, people are upset with the message, not the messenger. It takes time to develop a thick skin because we naturally want people to like us, however unrealistic that may be.

## Audience Expectations

When planning a presentation, another vital piece of information is knowing how long you're supposed to speak. Many community groups and staff meetings run on a tight schedule, so the meeting planner should be able to give you a specific time limit. If none has been set, think about the type of presentation you're making. A welcome or an introduction of another speaker should last only a couple of minutes — five maximum. And unless you're delivering a seminar, most other speeches should last only 10 to 20 minutes — 30 at the most. Audiences lose interest quickly. Adult attention is generally around 12 to 20 minutes.

Two rules of thumb are:

- **Rule of 20:** Every 20 minutes (maximum) exercise or summarize.

- **2-4 Minute Rule:** Do a "pattern interrupt" (move, change, shift) every 2-4 minutes.

Also consider if your presentation is formal or informal, follows a discussion or lecture format, or includes specific or overview information. This information will help you prepare a better presentation.

Even with a good presentation, don't expect your audience to be on the edge of their seat the whole time. The truth is that people will mentally come and go all throughout your speech. That's because:

- People's attention spans are short.

- They constantly shift.

- They are widely selective.

Here are four "pattern interrupts" for bringing back your audience mentally.

1. **Vary your intensity.** Your emotional impact shouldn't be the same throughout your presentation. In some spots, you'll want to be cool, calm and collected. In others, you'll want to raise your voice and pound your fist for emphasis.

2. **Move around.** There's nothing more boring than a speaker who stands in one place with his arms at his side.

3. **Keep your material relevant.** The audience always wants to know: What's in it for me? The longer you meet people's needs, the longer you'll keep their attention.

4. **Vary your voice.** This includes your volume, your content and how fast you speak. Just keep in mind the audience you're talking to. With children, content is important because they need to understand your words. While addressing a group of older adults in a care center, you might have to speak more loudly so they can hear you. And when it comes to rate of speech, North Americans speak at an average of anywhere between 125 to 250 words per minute. That means you may want to talk slower or faster, depending on the group you're addressing.

## Attention Flow Charts

Every presentation has three parts: initiation (introduction), involvement (body), and closure. The following four flow charts, which are divided into these three parts, represent four different presentations. The curved line in each chart indicates the energy and involvement required to maintain attention.

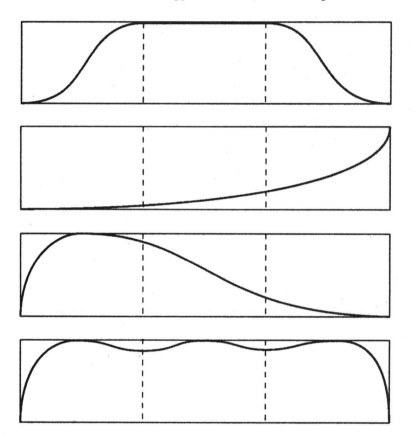

In the first flow chart, the presenter wants to achieve the greatest audience impact in his involvement section. His presentation starts slowly, peaks in the middle and then drops off at the end. By engaging the audience in the body, he maintains attention for his instructional points.

The second attention flow chart represents a motivational or inspirational speech, perhaps even a sales pitch. The presenter starts out slowly and then builds to a climax. The excites the audience and gets them ready to take action.

If you're giving just a short presentation or introducing another speaker or someone at a dinner, include all your important information at the beginning. This is the model shown in the third energy chart. Your goal is to grab the audience's attention early and end on a low note. This way you don't steal the next speaker's thunder or step on his toes.

Many longer presentations look like the last energy chart, with both peaks and valleys. When putting your presentation together, you should plan where your main points, zingers, stories and jokes — the peaks — will come. These keep the audience interested and involved. However, your presentation also will have a few valleys — places where the audience may become bored or begin to drift away mentally. Taking their energy up and down will keep them with you.

In fact, professional speakers often make a flow chart for each presentation they give and keep it handy while speaking. That way, they anticipate where the audience will lose interest, but they also know when a hook is coming up to draw people back into their speech. (Some even jot down the time between these peaks and valleys.) For example, your audience may wander off while you recite some mundane facts and figures, but they'll snap to attention when you start to tell a funny story about how someone misunderstood those same facts and figures. After you know your content, add the peaks — carefully and deliberately.

You can plan peaks by framing each 12 to 20 minutes of your presentation. Include a transition, plan hooks (humor, a quote or statistic) tell them what's in it for them, and give them some application ideas. This preparation will keep them with you.

The next time you're asked to speak to a group, use the following questions to help prepare your presentation.

1. How many people will be in the group?

2. Whom will I be speaking to? Superiors? Peers? Subordinates? A special-interest group? A specific industry?

3. How can I best meet their needs?

4. How should I deal with a potentially hostile audience?

5. How long am I expected to speak?

6. Should the presentation be formal or informal, follow a discussion or lecture format, or include specific or overview information?

7. What can I do to keep my audience interested throughout most of my presentation?

# Reflections

## Summary

Everyone is a presenter at one time or another. So, when it's your turn, get off to a good start by being creative and imaginative. Because people will judge you and draw conclusions about you even before you open your mouth, focus on your dress, mood, tone and expertise. These are really the only things you can control.

Good presentations have five important elements: arrangement, sources, style, memory and delivery. People judge you by your self-presentation, connection and positioning.

Always do an audience analysis before preparing your presentation. This includes taking into consideration both the size of the group and its makeup. There are basically three group sizes:

1.  One to 10 people — an intimate group

2.  11 to 50 people — a small group

3.  51+ people — a large group

Depending on its size, your dynamics or interaction with the audience should change. Also be sure you know who'll be in the audience and tailor your message accordingly. In a work-related setting, it could be your superiors, peers, subordinates or a combination of the three. In other cases, you may be talking to a special-interest group. Try to determine ahead of time if you'll face a hostile audience and how to handle it.

Also plan the energy level you want throughout your entire presentation, knowing that:

*   People's attention spans are short.

*   They constantly shift.

*   They are widely selective.

You can keep them centered and listening to key points throughout.

To regain your audience's attention, follow these suggestions:

1. Vary your intensity.

2. Move around.

3. Keep your material relevant.

4. Vary your voice.

Every presentation can be diagrammed using a flow chart. Its curved line represents how an audience's energy and involvement will come and go during a particular presentation. Many professional speakers make a flow chart so they can anticipate where an audience might lose interest and where it'll regain its attention. They then frame their presentation, planning where to pump energy in through transitions, hooks, application pieces and benefit statements.

Planning for success will cause it. Remember Mark Twain's comment, *"The difference between a presentation and a great presentation is like the difference between lightning and a lightning bug."*

# 2 IDENTIFY YOUR PRESENTATION STYLE

After reading this chapter you will know:

- what kind of a presenter you are

- how to present to different types of people

- how to stay out of the Gray Zone

What kind of a presenter are you? Red Zone, Blue Zone, Gray Zone or probably somewhere in between? These colors are code words that describe how you come off when speaking before a group. In most instances, your presentation style somewhat mirrors your personality.

A Blue-Zone presenter captures your attention through clearheaded persuasiveness. These very smart people fill their heads with data, facts and figures. They're analytical, logical, pragmatic, thoughtful, deliberate, rational, restrained, intellectual and insightful. Some examples of Blue-Zone presenters include former Secretary of State Henry Kissinger, former Ambassador to the United Nations Jeane Kirkpatrick, consumer advocate Ralph Nader and commentator William F. Buckley. Folks like these don't smile a lot; they come armed with information and let you have it.

In contrast, a Red-Zone presenter is full of energy and enthusiasm. Her adrenaline never stops flowing. You could hang a sign on a Red-Zone presenter that says, "You may not like me, but you can't ignore me." These people are emotional, driven, surprising, instinctive, charismatic, creative, impulsive, daring and disjointed. Some better-known Red-Zone presenters are former Presidents Ronald Reagan and John F. Kennedy, the Rev. Jesse Jackson and comedienne Joan Rivers.

Then you have the Gray-Zone presenters. They would rather be safe and bland than take a risk that might make them look foolish. Just remember if you're too neutral, too cautious, or too ambivalent, then you probably also put audiences to sleep. Unfortunately, most speakers fall into this category. In addition to neutral, cautious and ambivalent, Gray-Zone presenters tend to be traditional, accommodating, compromising, predictable, noncommittal and, especially, boring.

## Personality Assessment

To help determine your own speaking style, take the following Personality Assessment that contains 20 questions. There are no good or bad, or right or wrong answers. Simply select the answer that seems closest to how you view yourself. Put a check mark or an X in the box after the phrase that best describes you.

## A Personality Assessment — Who Am I?

|  | Extrovert | Introvert | Judger | Perceiver |
|---|---|---|---|---|

1. At a party, do you: .................................
   a. Talk to many, including strangers?...[ ]
   b. Talk to a few known to you? .........................[ ]
2. Do you make selections:
   a. Carefully?.....................................................[ ]
   b. Somewhat impulsively?.........................................[ ]
3. Before making a phone call, do you:
   a. Rarely think about the details?.........[ ]
   b. Rehearse what you'll say? ............................[ ]
4. Do you place more emphasis on:
   a. The definite? ...............................................[ ]
   b. The possible? .................................................[ ]
5. Do you prefer:
   a. Many friends with brief contact? .....[ ]
   b. Few friends with lengthy contact?.................[ ]
6. Are you more:
   a. Serious and determined?.............................[ ]
   b. Easygoing?.......................................................[ ]
7. Choose one from each word pair that best describes you:
   a. Social ...............................[ ]
   b. Territorial ......................................[ ]

   a. Settled ...........................................[ ]
   b. Pending ...........................................................[ ]

   a. Expend.................................[ ]
   b. Conserve ......................................[ ]

   a. Planner ..........................................[ ]
   b. Adapter .............................................................[ ]

   a. Broad ...............................[ ]
   b. Deep ..............................................[ ]

|  | Extrovert | Introvert | Judger | Perceiver |
|---|---|---|---|---|
| a. Fixed | | | [ ] | |
| b. Flexible | | | | [ ] |
| a. Extensive | [ ] | | | |
| b. Intensive | | [ ] | | |
| a. Decisive | | | [ ] | |
| b. Tentative | | | | [ ] |
| a. Interaction | [ ] | | | |
| b. Concentration | | [ ] | | |
| a. Closed | | | [ ] | |
| b. Open-ended | | | | [ ] |

8. Do you:
   a. Hurry to answer the phone first?......[ ]
   b. Hope someone else will answer?...................[ ]

9. Are you more:
   a. Deliberate than spontaneous? ......................[ ]
   b. Spontaneous than deliberate? ...................................[ ]

10. Are you:
    a. Easy to approach?..........................[ ]
    b. Somewhat reserved? ......................................[ ]

11. Are you more:
    a. Routine than whimsical?......................................[ ]
    b. Whimsical than routine?...........................................[ ]

12. At parties do you:
    a. Stay late with increasing energy?.....[ ]
    b. Leave early with decreased energy?..............[ ]

13. Does it bother you more having things:
    a. Incomplete?...................................................[ ]
    b. Complete?.............................................................[ ]

14. Do you:
    a. Anticipate conversation?..................[ ]
    b. Wait to be approached?.................................[ ]

|  | Extrovert | Introvert | Judger | Perceiver |
|---|---|---|---|---|

15. In your daily schedule do you:
    a.   Seek order? ..................................................................[  ]
    b.   Take things as they come?.............................................[  ]
16. Do changes in daily events:
    a.   Stimulate and energize you?.............[  ]
    b.   Tax your reserves? ..............................[  ]
17. Are you more comfortable:
    a.   After a decision?........................................................[  ]
    b.   Before a decision? ......................................................[  ]
18. Which saying best typifies you in each pair:
    a.   Let's talk........................................[  ]
    b.   Let me think....................................[  ]

    a.   Deadline!........................................................[  ]
    b.   What deadline? ...............................................[  ]
19. Do you:
    a.   Overstate something to make a point?  [  ]
    b.   Understate something to be sure?..................[  ]
20. Which best typifies you?
    a.   Get the show on the road!..........................................[  ]
    b.   Let's wait and see ..........................................................[  ]

**Scoring:** Add up the number of check marks or X's you've placed in each of the four columns and record that total.  None of these numbers should be larger than 15.  In fact, the total of columns one and two should equal 15, and so should the total of columns three and four.  As you can see, the first column indicates your extrovert score, the second your introvert score, the third your judger score and the fourth your perceiver score.  Compare columns one and two.  The column with the larger number represents your preferred personality style.  Now do the same with columns three and four.  The column with the larger number represents how you make decisions.

No one style is better than the other.  This exercise isn't meant to change you, but to help you understand yourself and identify your tendencies.  Having this information will make you a better presenter.

## Different Styles for Different Folks

Generally, introverts are shy, detailed, reserved, meticulous, perfectionistic and risk-avoiders. During presentations, they appear reserved and thorough. According to National Seminars' research, about 35 percent of North Americans claim to be introverts.

The other 65 percent tend to be extroverts, who, by nature, are friendly, sociable, competitive and risk-takers. During presentations, they're outgoing and persuasive.

A judger is decisive and stubborn. She doesn't give others a chance to challenge her. When wrapping up a presentation, a judger might say, "Based on my research and my conclusions, this is what we will do. Any questions?"

On the other end of the spectrum is the perceiver, who tends to be flexible, tentative and more easily influenced. At the end of a presentation, a perceiver might say, "Based on my research, this is what I think we should do, unless anyone else has other suggestions."

When making decisions, sometimes we need to be decisive like the judger and other times flexible like the perceiver. It just depends upon the situation. According to National Seminars' research, the North American population is about evenly split between judgers and perceivers.

## How to Stay Out of the Gray Zone

Remember that most presenters fall into the Gray Zone. To be a truly effective and influential presenter, you must stay out of this zone. Following are some techniques that will help you.

1. **Show them — don't just tell them.** Whenever possible, use visual aids, such as charts, graphs, diagrams and photos.

2. **Don't read from visual aids.** They aren't scripts; they should be supporting materials and reminders of your main messages. Instead, glance at them. There's nothing worse than listening to a

speaker who puts a transparency on an overhead projector, then turns around and continues with her back to the audience. After all, who's giving this presentation? The speaker or the overheads? And, what if the overheads are lost or forgotten, or the power goes off? That speaker will be lost without them.

3. **Move around — podiums can be poison.** Podiums act as barriers to your audience and security blankets for speakers. Some presenters get white knuckles from holding onto podiums for dear life! And when a short speaker hides behind one, sometimes all the audience can see is a head bobbing up and down behind the podium. Both of these situations are ridiculous! There may be times when you must stay behind a podium because it offers the only light in the room, you have to read some copy, or the presentation format calls for it, such as a debate. Unless you find yourself in one of these situations, try to move around — to the right, to the left, even out in front of the podium.

4. **Use two flip charts.** One should be for listing objectives for your presentation and the other for results. Using two charts also forces you to move between them.

5. **Don't imitate others — be yourself.** Each presenter is unique in one way or another, and that's what you should try to emphasize. It's how audiences will remember you. Once in a while it's all right to borrow material or emulate techniques used by other speakers. Everyone does that, even professional presenters. But don't become a clone of someone else. Find your own speaking strengths and project them.

6. **Mix the Red and Blue Zones for a better presentation.** Go for a balanced blend of facts and figures and enthusiasm and energy.

## A Balanced Presentation

Here's how to give a presentation that combines Red- and Blue-Zone presentation techniques. When an extrovert gives a presentation to a whole group of extroverts, there are lots of fun, games, jokes and role-playing. Everyone has a great time. However, if you did this with a group of introverts, you'd be seen as shallow and lacking substance. They want to know the data and research behind your words.

When an introvert speaks, she can recite all kinds of facts and figures. But if she's talking to a group made up of mostly extroverts — say, a group of sales managers — then she'll bore her audience to death. People may be looking at her and smiling, but their minds have wandered elsewhere.

Bottom line, sometimes you have to come out of your comfort zone — whether it's Red, Blue or Gray — to effectively speak to your audience. The best presenters do this all the time. They understand their audiences and vary their presentation styles to meet their audiences' needs and preferences.

How would you alter your presentation and presentation style to fit the following situations and types of audiences? Briefly explain the steps you would take in the spaces below.

1. Your boss has asked you to brief the Sales and Finance departments on the departmental hiring strategy. (Audience mix: 65% extroverts/35% introverts)

2. As a member of the Employee Participation Board, you are asked to speak to the company about the annual fund-raising campaign. (Audience mix: 90% extroverts/10% introverts)

3. As a community volunteer for the annual festival, you need to outline your goals for the coming year. (Audience mix: 25% extroverts/75% introverts)

# Reflections

## Summary

Presenters can be described according to three color code words: Red Zone, Blue Zone and Gray Zone.

A Blue-Zone presenter is filled with facts and figures. They're analytical, logical, pragmatic, thoughtful, deliberate, rational, restrained, intellectual and insightful. In contrast, a Red-Zone presenter is full of energy and enthusiasm. These people are emotional, driven, surprising, instinctive, charismatic, creative, impulsive, daring and disjointed.

Then there are the Gray-Zone presenters. To avoid risks that might make them look foolish, they come off as neutral, cautious, ambivalent, traditional, accommodating, compromising, predictable, noncommittal and, especially, boring.

Taking the Personality Assessment will help you determine your speaking style and make you a better speaker. Whether you're an extrovert or introvert, judger or perceiver, one is no better than the other.

Introverts tend to be shy, detailed, reserved, meticulous, perfectionistic and risk-avoiders. They appear reserved and thorough during presentations. In contrast, extroverts tend to be friendly, sociable, competitive and risk-takers. They're outgoing and persuasive during presentations. A judger is decisive and stubborn — someone who doesn't give others a chance to challenge her. Meanwhile the perceiver tends to be flexible, tentative and more easily influenced.

Although most presenters fall into the Gray Zone, try to stay out of it by following these six techniques:

1. Show them — don't just tell them.
2. Don't read from visual aids.
3. Move around — podiums can be poison.
4. Use two flip charts.
5. Don't imitate others — be yourself.
6. Mix the Red and Blue Zones for a better presentation.

# 3  KNOW YOUR SUBJECT

After reading this chapter you will know:

- how to prepare a presentation flow chart

- how to use three different presentation models

- when to accept a speaking engagement

You're sitting in the audience when the just-introduced speaker pulls a thick, typed manuscript out of his coat pocket. What's your reaction? Can't wait to hear what he has to say? Are you on the edge of your seat? Probably not. In most cases, you're trying to count how many pages of text he's going to read or you're wondering if he even wrote the speech himself.

A speaker who does this might as well record his speech at home or at the office, bring the tape to the function and play it there for everyone to hear. Then, after it's finished, he can ask the audience if there are any questions. Doesn't that seem simpler and maybe more interesting?

The point is, you should know your presentation material so well that you can give it by glancing at headlines or key phrases. Many speakers use index cards for this. And, one of the best ways to organize your notes is on a flow chart.

## Go with the Flow

Pictured on page 32 is a flow chart consisting of three inverted triangles — one each for your presentation's introduction, body and close. Within each triangle are the numbers one, two and three. Number one represents the things you must say during your presentation. Number two represents the things you should say, while number three represents the things you could say if you have enough time.

Excellent presentations are organized, flow logically, communicate meaning and maintain interest. Using a modular breakdown, you can adhere to the old adage:

*"tell 'em what you are going to tell 'em,*
*tell 'em, and tell 'em what you told them."*

The triangle model focuses the listener's attention. Structuring your presentation, whether five minutes or five hours, through the triangle model respects the following adult learning principles:

- **People remember most what they hear first.** So carefully create the introduction to let people know you are good and your message is worth it.

- **People remember best what they hear last.** Plan your close first, after identifying how you want the audience to be, do or feel at the end of your presentation.

Transitions, by which you summarize and then move to another point, support the adult learner's need for repetition.

Three tips to enhance the triangle formula:

1. **Decide what to say.** This is the *self-presentation* element. Great communicators may possess special information, but while content is important, real talent comes from delivery. Delivery is based upon well-organized material.

2. **Organize the talk.** This involves *positioning the information.* Simplicity, brevity, and awareness of your audience's condition, interests, and needs pinpoint what must be said versus what you could say. Always lead with what they will relate to.

3. **Focus attention.** This is done through the *connection* element. Start with issues of direct concern to the audience. Provide different ways to look at things. Give them a solution to their problem.

**TOPIC**

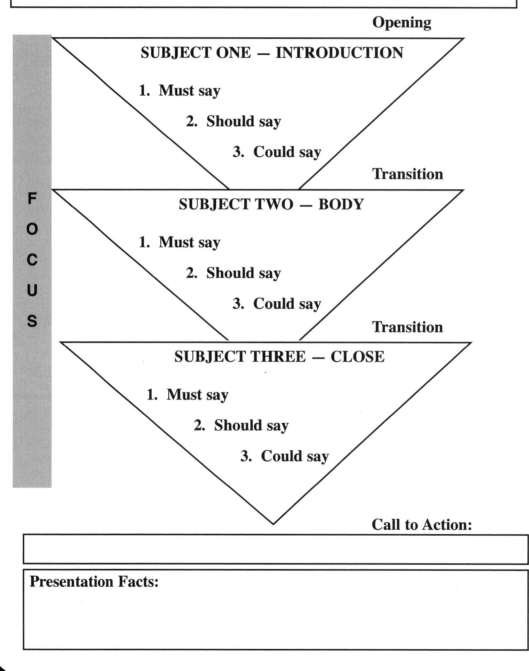

Opening

**SUBJECT ONE — INTRODUCTION**

1. Must say
2. Should say
3. Could say

Transition

**SUBJECT TWO — BODY**

1. Must say
2. Should say
3. Could say

Transition

**SUBJECT THREE — CLOSE**

1. Must say
2. Should say
3. Could say

**F O C U S**

**Call to Action:**

**Presentation Facts:**

By just glancing at these headlines or key phrases, you'll always know what comes next. If you have to briefly read something, do it. Then, immediately go back to the audience and resume eye contact. Because of the simplicity of the flow chart, you should never lose your place in your presentation.

What also makes the triangle model work so well is its flexibility. Say you've prepared a 30-minute presentation for a staff meeting. Just before you're ready to speak, you're told the meeting is running long so you need to cut it to 15 minutes. If you're using a plan, you can easily eliminate some of your "should say" or all of your "could say" material. There's no need to panic, because your presentation will still flow and have an opening, body and close. On the other hand, if you were prepared to read a 15-page speech, you'd be in big trouble trying to cut it at the last minute.

You'll notice that the module diagram also includes a transition between the introduction and body, and between the body and close of your presentation. A transition helps your material flow better and move from one subject to the next. Examples of good transitions are stories, jokes, illustrations, demonstrations and audience-participation tactics. For instance, if you're trying to recruit people for the American Red Cross blood drive, during the closing of your presentation you might tell a poignant story about how one pint of blood saved a person's life.

In the last module is your call to action. This is where you ask people to do something, give them a challenge or offer a solution to a problem. Using the previous example, you might ask audience members to sign up for their company's blood drive immediately after you finish your speech.

## Training Formats

**Standard Format**

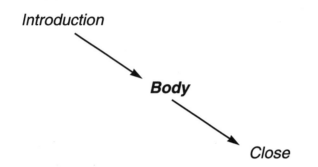

*Introduction*

**Body**

*Close*

**Frequently Used Openers**

- Definitions
- Rhetorical questions
- Humor
- Poem
- Historical reference
- Startling fact
- Current event
- Quote
- Personal experience
- Statistic
- Visual

**Frequently Used Body Formats**

- Lecture

- Discussion

- Audio presentations — music, audio tapes, singing

- Visual presentations —  PowerPoint, overheads, chalkboards, flip-charts, slides

- Audio-visual presentations — videos

- Games, exercises, quizzes, tests, case studies

**Frequently Used Closures**

- Lecture review

- Activity using the knowledge

- Tests and evaluations

Fill in the following flow chart with headlines or key phrases you might use when giving the quarterly sales report at your next staff meeting.

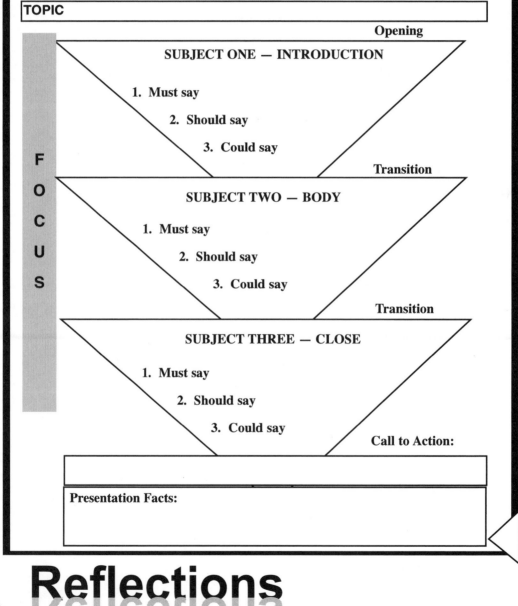

**TOPIC**

Opening

**F O C U S**

**SUBJECT ONE — INTRODUCTION**

1. Must say

2. Should say

3. Could say

Transition

**SUBJECT TWO — BODY**

1. Must say

2. Should say

3. Could say

Transition

**SUBJECT THREE — CLOSE**

1. Must say

2. Should say

3. Could say

Call to Action:

**Presentation Facts:**

# Reflections

## Presentation Facts

- **Know what's most important and say it.** Have your main points written down. You may need to communicate them more than once to get your point across.

- **Know what your audience needs and say it.** This will come from your audience analysis. Remember, the more you know about your audience, the better you'll be able to meet its needs.

- **A presentation should contain only a few simple, dynamic ideas or thoughts.** The key here is few, and the fewer the better. Don't try to cram too much into the time you've been allotted. Remember, it's very flattering when people ask you to tell them more.

- **The way you organize your speech determines what is heard.** It's always a good idea to have a strong open and close for your presentation. Just keep this tried-and-true rule in mind: People tend to remember best what they heard last; they tend to remember most what they heard first.

- **People listen to speakers for a while and then make mental side trips.** This is typical human behavior. Just accept it and try to deal with it as best you can.

- **Transitional techniques such as stories, jokes and demonstrations bring them back.** These are the best ways to regain your audience's attention.

- **Excessive facts, figures or details should be presented as handouts, preferably at the close of your speech.** As long as your audience doesn't need to refer to the handouts during your presentation, wait until afterwards to give them out. If handouts are distributed right before a presentation, people tend to pay more attention to them than you. Another option is to send your handouts to audience members a couple of days in advance. This allows them to review the material before your presentation.

- **Incite, don't inform.** Effective presentations don't end with nodding heads and polite applause. They end with action. The most important question to ask before any presentation is, "What do I want my audience to do and how do I convince them to do it?"

  The best presentations answer basic questions that few presenters ever bother asking: What's my core message? How does that message benefit my audience? What barriers are there to people accepting the message? What common ground (values, experience, goals) do I share with the audience? When I finish, what do I want the audience to do? Presentations are about objectives, benefits, and actions.

  Design slides as tools for persuasion rather than sources of information.

- **Don't talk to strangers.** Conduct informal research a few days before a presentation. You should know as much as you can about who you're speaking to. What are their expectations? Where are they positioned on the issue? What's their knowledge level? What are their demographics and cultures?

Remember, first (and last) impressions are everything. Every presentation guru makes the same point: the two most important parts of your presentation are the first 30 and the last 15 seconds. People make a decision in the first 30 seconds about whether they're going to listen to you.

A powerful close leaves the audience with something of value and relates directly to the opening. If you opened with a story, complete the story at the close. If you opened with a statistic or quote, restate it at the end.

A final point on which the experts agree is that presenters should always finish early.

## Three Presentation Models

When planning your presentation, there are three methods to use. The diagram below helps explain each.

1. The Deductive Model is a lecture format.

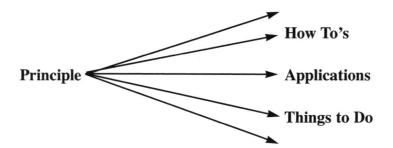

2. The Inductive Model is participative.

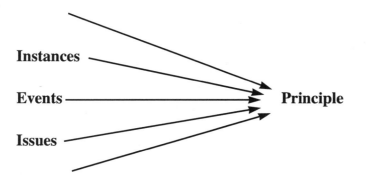

3. The Combination Model is lecture, participative, and discussion.

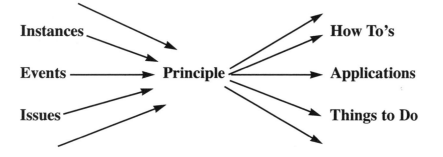

1. **The Deductive Presentation.** This presentation, which is the shortest and easiest to give, follows a lecture format. You begin with a basic principle and then deliver its how to's, applications and things that must be done. An example would be setting higher quotas for next quarter for members of your sales staff and then telling them how to meet their new goals.

2. **The Inductive Presentation.** This model flows in the opposite direction because it involves the audience or requires group participation. It's perfect for brainstorming or strategy-building sessions. Because more people are talking, an inductive presentation takes more time. As a result of discussing issues, events and instances, together you reach a consensus, solve a problem or establish a principle. Using the previous example, members of your sales staff might discuss the instances, events and issues facing them in the current marketplace and come up with new quotas they think are fair and attainable.

3. **The Combination Presentation.** Since this model is both deductive and inductive, it requires even more time. As a presenter, you rely on ideas and input from the group or audience to reach a consensus or set a principle. At that point, then you, as boss or committee chair, tell them what needs to be done or how to apply what has been discussed. Continuing with the same example, you would talk with your sales staff, together set new quotas and then explain how staffers should go about meeting them.

Every time you speak you need to determine which model will work best with your audience and which will have the most impact. Ask yourself, "Will people get more out of my presentation if I lecture them, if I allow them input, or if I give them a little bit of both?"

## Divide Your Development Time

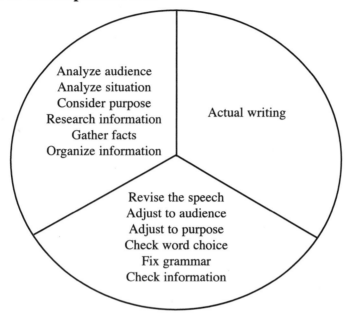

Steps for preparing the presentation include:

- Formulate topic, define purpose, think of ideas.
- Gather materials, research, organize thoughts.
- Write the close.
- Write the introduction.
- Draft the body.
- Add stories, humor, anecdotes.
- Tailor presentation to audience.
- Develop visual support.
- Determine timing.
- Evaluate presentation and measure against goal.
- Try out presentation and get feedback.
- Edit: check for flow, relevance, connection.

You can begin a presentation in a variety of ways. Be creative. Go from the familiar to the unfamiliar. Make the audience participants, not spectators; for example, interject with "Imagine you are in a ..." or tell a story — "A funny thing happened ... ." Acknowledge the occasion and the audience; for example, begin with "This is the first ... ." Or pay the listeners a compliment. An example would be, "I have worked with ... and admired ... ." Make a striking statement with something like, "Our company could become ... ." Use an unusual statistic like "If all our unhappy customers held hands, we would have a chain around the perimeter of a football field." Refer to a statement made by a previous speaker. You might say, "Before I begin, I want to comment on what John said ..."

Other possibilities might be to ask a challenging question, like "What is the most common cause of business failure today?" Ask for a show of hands on a topic; "How many here today believe ... ?" Establish credibility by inserting examples of relevant experience: "I was speaking to an audience of investment bankers last week ... ." Make a promise; for example, you might offer to share a beneficial idea in the upcoming minutes. Start with visuals, such as a two-minute video, projection materials or multimedia.

The conclusion should summarize the presentation, provide closure and make a final impression. You can cue the audience by saying, "Turning now to my final points ... ." You could refer back to the opening by returning to the intro story or anecdote. In conclusion, summarize the presentation; for example say, "In summary, there are five ways we can keep our customers forever ..." or ask a question like, "Will we put customers first?"

You can close with an anecdote: "Let me conclude by telling you about a fellow worker who ..." or tell a story, a legend, myth or happening that exemplifies the point of the talk. Reciting a poem is effective: "I should like to close with the immortal words of Richard Goodwin: 'I really love a finished speaker. I really truly do. I don't mean one who's polished. I just mean one who's through.' "

Try ending on humor, "Thank you and God bless you. And now the words you have been waiting for: Let's eat." (Ronald Reagan)

You can tell the audience what to do: "Get behind this plan and ... ." You can ask for help — "With your support, we can ..."; make an admission — "We must ask these questions today ..."; or call for action — "Call your congressional representative ... ," etc.

Transitions gain and hold audience attention. They lead the audience from one section or idea to another. They can provide internal summaries. Also, they let the audience know where they are, where they have been and where they are going throughout the presentation. Some examples include:

- "Today I will discuss the three reasons for ... First ... Second ..."

- "To summarize these points ..."

- "In the last example ... Next I'll show you how ..."

- "... and just as with that ... so is it with ..."

Transitions can be attention-grabbers to:

- Get the audience involved. Secure active participation and cooperation as quickly as possible.

- Keep them guessing. Arouse curiosity with baffling questions that seem to lack solutions, like brainteasers and riddles.

- Tell stories. Illustrate main themes and points through narratives that work with the material.

- Make your point with visuals. Bring presentations to life with variety, color, imagination.

- Present them with a problem. Make it challenging yet solvable, in order to get active participation.

- Carry them smoothly. Ensure transitions flow logically.

## To Speak or Not to Speak?

It's an important question: Should you always accept an invitation to speak? No, not always. In some cases, you might not have a choice — especially if your boss is doing the asking. However, you should consider declining the request if you can't honestly agree with all three of these statements:

1. I've earned the right to talk about the subject.

2. I'm excited about the subject.

3. I'm eager to share this information with others.

Here's another checklist that will help you determine if you should speak. You might want to laminate this list so you can refer to it both before and after deciding to give a presentation. It's also useful when evaluating how well your presentation went.

### Before Accepting a Speaking Engagement

Am I the right person for this occasion?

- How will I be perceived by the audience?

- My credibility to speak comes from:

Do I have a message to send to this audience?

- My main point is:

- The thing I want my audience to do is:

Do I have the time commitments to do the job right?

- Preparation time needed:

- Time allotted to present materials:

**Once I Accept a Speaking Engagement**

Do I have a plan for delivery?

- Style:

- Content:

- Interaction:

Am I adequately prepared?

- Am I properly organized?

- Am I emotionally and mentally ready?

- Are my support materials ready?

What kind of response do I anticipate?

How will I assure that I'm heard?

Will my presentation be accepted in the spirit it's intended?

**After I Finish My Presentation**

Did I accomplish my purpose?

Do I have valid feedback about my presentation?

How far did I divert from my plan?

What could I have done better?

What worked well?

Do I need to do anything as a follow-up?

Novice presenters often ask if they should turn down a speech just because it will require them to do some research. The answer is no. You should always do at least a little research to prepare a presentation, but only enough to support what you already know.

For example, most of us would have to decline a speaking engagement about how a computer processor works. Only people trained in advanced technology understand that. However, if you're an experienced computer user, with some additional research you could probably teach your sales staff how to use its new spreadsheet software.

The additional knowledge gained through research will make you more credible, better prepared and, in the long run, a better speaker.

## Summary

You should know your presentation material so well that you can give it by glancing at a few headlines or key phrases. A flow chart consisting of three inverted triangles — one each for your presentation's introduction, body and close — will help you do that. Within each triangle are the numbers one, two and three. Number one represents the things you must say, number two represents the things you should say, and number three represents the things you could say.

Using the triangle model makes your presentation flexible, especially if you have to cut several minutes from it.

A modular organization also features a transition between the introduction and body, and between the body and close of a presentation. Transitions, which help your material flow better, include stories, jokes, illustrations, demonstrations and audience-participation tactics. At the very end of the last module is your call to action.

When planning a presentation, there are three methods to use. Before you speak, determine which will work best with your audience.

The Deductive Model is a lecture format. Here you present the principle, your theme or main point, and then present applications for that point. There is little opportunity for questions or discussion. This is the easiest method to use and one most audiences prefer since it is easy to follow. An example is, "We must decrease costs. To do that, we … ."

The Inductive Model is a more flexible presentation structure. It is good for use with group participation. It allows the audience to determine the principle or point through questions and discussion. It starts with pieces and builds a case. It is preferred by creative, innovative people. An example, "We must decrease costs. What ways can you suggest to do that?"

The Combination Model takes longer and requires greater audience participation. You present instances, events or issues and allow the audience to determine the principle. You then present the applications. Some audiences find this tedious. For example, a group of executives may want to get to the point quickly. An example of this model is: "We must decrease costs. What ways can you suggest to do that? Now based on what you've suggested, this is what we must do to decrease our costs … ."

Regardless of which model you choose, speak to the audience's whole brain. Mix and mingle facts and statements with stories and emotion. Taking people back and forth in their brain triggers buy in, memory and enjoyment.

How much is enough? Churchill once commented: "When you say all you have to say and come to a grammatically correct end, sit down."

An old adage to remember is:

- know your stuff
- know who you are stuffing
- know when they are stuffed

Remember, it isn't necessary to accept every speaking engagement. Of course, if it's your boss doing the asking, you might not have a choice. However, consider declining the request if you can't honestly agree with all three of these statements:

1. I've earned the right to talk about the subject.

2. I'm excited about the subject.

3. I'm eager to share this information with others.

When preparing a presentation, you should always do some research, but only enough to support what you already know.

# 4 PRESENTING YOUR MATERIALS

After reading this chapter you will know:

- what audiences like and dislike

- how to build rapport with your audience

- how to effectively use humor in your presentations

Do you know what audiences like and dislike? Do you know what turns an audience on and what turns an audience off? As presenters, it's easy to forget what it feels like to be out there in the audience where there's no pressure to perform.

Here are a few reminders to keep you in good standing with your audience.

## Audience Likes

1. **Deal tactfully with disruptions.** If two people seem to be giving their own presentation somewhere in the room, the best way to deal with this distraction is to quit talking. Your silence will be magical. All of the attention in the room suddenly will shift to these two, who will quickly quiet down.

2. **Be physically direct.** Move toward audience members, make direct eye contact with individuals and increase the volume of your voice. If you don't move, you'll look stiff. At the same time, if

you move too fast or get too close, you'll make people uncomfortable, so find a happy medium. The same rule applies to eye contact. Split-second glances make you look shifty and not very credible or believable. Instead, focus on each person for about three seconds, just long enough to build rapport. Staring at people too long — say 20 to 30 seconds — can make them uncomfortable. As for your voice, keep it sounding good-natured and pleasant. In many cases, these physical elements — your movement, eye contact and voice — will make or break your presentation.

3. **Be friendly.** If you come across as a friendly speaker, your audience will be friendly too. People tend to reflect your attitude and manner. For instance, call people by name when it's appropriate. Seasoned speaker Dale Carnegie once said, "A person's name is the sweetest and most important sound in any language." And, don't forget to smile when it's appropriate. After all, it takes fewer muscles to smile than to frown.

## Audience Dislikes

1. **Cleverness or clichés.** This is where many speakers go overboard. It's okay to be a little clever or use a couple of clichés, as long as you don't overdo it. With clichés, the audience always knows what you're going to say before you say it. How many times have you heard, "You can't judge a book by its cover" or "If you can't stand the heat, get out of the kitchen"?

2. **Sermonizing.** Unless you're a member of the clergy, avoid morally instructing your audience. Someone who acts so perfect and so pious is a real audience turn-off.

3. **A "teachy" style.** This includes being overpatronizing or talking down to your audience. Teachers and parents tend to do this.

4. **Being too loud too early.** Don't begin your presentation by blasting audience members out of their seats. You should build up to this point, if you ever reach it at all. One exception may be

during a meeting when you need to tap on a glass, ring a bell or rap a gavel to get people's attention.

5. **Constant hard driving.** If you continually pound away at your audience, you never give members a chance to catch their breath or reflect on what you're saying. Besides, it might give them all headaches.

6. **Mismatching language and content.** This happens when your words don't go along with what you're talking about. When giving a presentation on a particular subject, you have to "know how to speak the language." And virtually every profession or industry has its own vocabulary. For instance, if you're speaking to a group of computer technicians, then you had better use and understand their technological terms. If you don't, you're sure to lose your audience.

Some no-no's in public speaking include:

- Talking too rapidly

- Speaking in a monotone

- Using too high a vocal pitch

- Not smiling enough while talking

- Talking and not saying much

- Presenting without enough emotion or passion

- Using too many big words

- Using abstractions without giving concrete examples

- Not explaining the meaning of words and expressions

- Using unfamiliar technical jargon

- Not introducing the message and its relevance clearly

- Using poor grammar

- Talking without preparation or knowledge of the topic

- Disorganized and rambling performance

- Not making proper eye contact with listeners

- Fidgety behavior that distracts the listeners

- Talking down to the audience

- Indirect communication, beating around the bush

- Not summarizing and concluding the message clearly

- Failing to use visual aids to illustrate points

- Insulting the audience's intelligence

- Not asking for action

There are several strategies you can use to improve the quality of a presentation:

- Repetitive phrases

  — Monitor yourself for commonly repeated phrases.

- Excessive vocal pauses

  — Listen to a presentation, identify the uhs, and develop signals to flag their usage.

- No pauses or lengthy pauses

  — Use the power of a well-placed two-second pause.

- Mentally test phrases and ideas, imagining the reaction.

  — Edit out or change threatening or easily misunderstood statements.

- Practice aloud to avoid overkill.

  — Tape a speech to identify proper word emphasis.

- Keep listeners' backgrounds and frame of reference in mind.

  — Imagine perceptions and reactions and set them up.

- Listen to both yourself and the reaction of the audience.

  — If you make a slip of the tongue or factual mistake, make it humorous, point it out yourself.

- Be attentive to negative audience reaction.

  — If people are disturbed, admit the mistake.

- Anticipate potential problems.

  — If you know of a possible negative, note it and go on.

- Identify the cheerleaders in the audience.

  — Talk to the people who are supportive, positive or attentive.

## Building Rapport

There's more to presenting than just standing in front of people and talking. Good speakers build rapport with their audiences; they have the ability to establish a relationship with them, often in just a couple of minutes.

Hopefully, you'll know all about your audience before you accept a speaking engagement. Doing an audience analysis or talking to the person who's setting up your presentation should help you determine how to best relate to people. However, there may be times when you can't do this. If that's the case, try these two techniques:

1. **Test the temperature.** Ask audience members some questions to learn more about them and to gauge their interest. If you were trying to recruit volunteers for the Red Cross blood drive, you

might say, "Let's get to know each other a little better. How many of you have ever donated blood before? How many of you have a close friend or family member who regularly donates blood? How many of you are terrified at the very thought of donating blood?" By asking people questions like these, you'll have a better idea of what to include in your presentation.

2. **Warm up the audience.** Always be open, friendly and excited when you first greet your audience. Many professional speakers use warm-up exercises to get things started on the right note. One example is to ask people to introduce themselves and say something about what they do. Another variation is to have people pair up, talk for about five minutes and then introduce each other to the rest of the audience. Both are common warm-up exercises that help shut down people's "carryover tapes" and prepare them to hear what you have to say. Just remember that warm-up exercises require some time, so they're not suitable for short presentations.

It's important to realize that you and your audience need each other. When people come to hear you speak, it's usually because they need to do something or they need help with an issue affecting them either at home or at work. As a speaker, you can't do your job without an audience.

Have you ever given what you thought was a great presentation, but the audience seemed a bit bored? It's probably because you were talking to yourself, rather than the people in your audience. Your material needs to be relevant and meet their needs. It's simply human nature for people to ask: "What's in it for me?" As a speaker, you have to continually ask yourself: "What's in it for them?" Test your information with "So what?" and "Who cares?"

Besides 2- and 3-year-olds who haven't learned differently yet, speakers can be the most selfish people in the world. Some drone on and on about what they've done, where they've been, who they know and how much money they earn. Talk like this bores an audience to death. Always put the needs and interests of your audience first. Always consider what the audience wants, not what you prefer.

## How to Use Humor

Since everyone loves to laugh, one of the very best ways to build rapport with your audience is through humor. This includes everything from jokes to riddles to true stories about human behavior. (In many cases, truth is funnier than fiction.)

David Kearns, chairman and chief executive officer of Xerox Corporation, told this joke as he addressed students at the University of Chicago Graduate School of Business (Kushner, 1990):

*"There's a story about a Frenchman, a Japanese and an American who face a firing squad. Each gets one last request. The Frenchman asks to hear 'The Marseillaise.' The Japanese asks to give a lecture on the art of management. The American says, 'Shoot me first — I can't stand one more lecture on Japanese management.'"*

After the laughter subsided he added, *"You'll be glad to hear I'm not going to talk about Japanese management today. In fact, if we keep on the right track, we may wind up listening to the Japanese give lectures on American management."* (Kushner, 1990, p. 39

Just as the message delivered was an important one, the messages that you deliver — whether in formal speaking engagements, in training sessions, or in informal conversations with trainees or clients — are equally important. If your message is worthwhile but boring, the chances are that it will not be heard, understood, and remembered. Humor enlivens your message and helps listeners to relax and pay attention. Gene Perret (1990), one of America's leading comedy writers, reinforces this point:

*"Some people may wonder 'why bother using humor when you can make a point as fiercely as possible and get on with it?' Marshall McLuhan answers with: 'Those who draw the distinction between education and entertainment don't know the first thing about either.'"*

An example of the benefits of humor come from Mario Cuomo:

*"As I left home to come down here tonight, my wife gave me some last-minute advice. She said, 'I know it's a difficult subject and a tough group, but don't be intimidated. And don't try to be charming, witty or intellectual. Just be yourself.'"*

Here are some ground rules for adding humor to your presentations.

1. **Use humor that fits your style.** While everyone loves to laugh, not everyone tells jokes very well. If your style is more low-key, don't force the hilarity. It won't work. Go for light stories or even self-deprecating humor. Former U.S. Senator Bob Dole is a master at this.

2. **Use humor that fits the occasion.** If the occasion is more serious in nature, then forget the jokes and instead tell a story that elicits a smile rather than a laugh.

3. **Use humor that fits the audience.** What's funny to one group may insult another. For instance, if you're speaking to a group of doctors, then you probably wouldn't want to tell a joke about medical malpractice. However, a group of lawyers might find the same joke extremely funny.

4. **Use humor as a recess.** Think of it as a break in the action. Especially during some meetings or long presentations, people become tense, uptight and mentally tired. Saying something humorous can break the mood and loosen everyone up.

5. **Make light of jokes that don't go well.** Speakers often tell jokes at the beginning of their presentations because it helps relieve some of their nervousness and breaks the ice with audiences. However, if your joke doesn't go over very well try saying, "If you hated that one, I've got 10 more just like it." That comeback will probably make them laugh. Late-night talk-show host Johnny Carson used this technique successfully. Don't worry when people don't laugh, deal with it and go on.

6. **Use humor as a bridge or transition.** Jokes and stories effectively allow you to move from one subject to another.

Demonstrating a sense of humor decreases the distance between you and your listeners and increases their trust in you. Listeners tend to develop a quicker rapport with a speaker who encourages laughter than with one who is serious and stern. Also listeners who laugh experience certain physiological and psychological reactions that not only benefit them but also benefit you, as a speaker seeking receptivity. Their facial, torso, and stomach muscles relax; their blood pressure goes down; and a general sense of well-being and euphoria takes over.

Research on the psychology of humor shows that humor has a rejuvenating effect on listeners. Regardless of how accomplished a speaker is, listeners eventually reach a saturation point at which they demand some refreshment or they will absorb no more. A little comedy can provide that refreshment, after which people can listen with renewed interest.

The link between fun and effectiveness is illustrated by Paul Hawken:

*"If you aren't having some fun, you might wonder just what you are doing in your business life ... If employees, customers, and vendors don't laugh and have a good time at your company, something is wrong."*

As Hawken implies in the preceding quote, there is a definite link between fun and effectiveness.

Think about how you would build rapport in the following speaking situations. Briefly explain how you might warm up your audience, how you would meet their needs and how you would incorporate appropriate humor into each presentation.

1. You must present financials to your boss and other executives.

2. You are to explain the annual fund-raising strategy to your civic organization.

3. You are to make a presentation to a high school on your company's activities and career opportunities.

Reflections
Reflections

## Dealing with Interruptions

It's inevitable. You're in the middle of a presentation and someone raises her hand to ask a question or challenge something you've said.

To cut down on interruptions, offer a disclaimer at the beginning of your presentation to keep it from happening in the first place. Say something like, "I'll be speaking for 20 minutes or so, and then I'll open it up for questions afterward. Is that okay with everyone?" Then when someone interrupts you, politely and diplomatically say, "That's the first question we'll deal with in the question-and-answer portion of the presentation."

Hopefully that last comment will head off any further interruptions. If the person stops you again, you can ask that she write her concern down for the question-and-answer time. Thank her and move on.

## Different Learning Styles

Did you know that each person takes in information in one of three different ways? Say you're explaining how to use a new computer software package. Some will do best if you give them handouts or an instruction manual. These are visual learners. Others will want you to tell them how to do it. These are auditory learners. The last group — the sensory learners — will succeed simply by using the computer; you talk, they do. They learn by touch and feel.

As a speaker, you have to appeal to all three kinds of learners because you'll find all three in your audiences. Here are some suggestions:

1. **Visual learners.** Use these kinds of phrases: "That looks good to me" or "I see what you mean." Provide them with lots of visual aids during your presentation. Remember, "A picture is worth a thousand words." Use printed materials, charts and diagrams.

2. **Auditory learners.** They respond to, "That sounds good to me" or "I hear what you're saying." Use variations in your voice as well as descriptive words and phrases to tell them what they need to

know. Add audiotapes or music to augment the lecture. Speak slowly and distinctly.

3. **Sensory learners.** They prefer phrases such as, "That feels good to me" or "I can't seem to put my finger on the problem." To help them learn, put something in their hands or give them something to do. Games, role-playing and all types of audience participation work well with sensory learners. Add requests for them to stand, turn to something or write something down.

## Presentation Facts

- **Acknowledge the host.** This can allow you to connect immediately.

- **Be sincere.** A genuine compliment given to your audience also causes rapport. Passion and emotion are real hooks.

- **Pay attention to your audience's opinions.** As a result, you may want to alter your presentation a bit.

- **Refer to an idea or event that is dominant in the mind of the audience.** To ignore it would suggest ignorance on your part. For instance, if a tragic news event has just taken place, acknowledge that everyone is thinking about it. Use the precall to neutralize potential problems.

- **Minimize differences at the beginning.** Find common ground with your audiences. If you try hard enough, you can always agree on something — even that the weather is lousy.

- **Skillfully compare and contrast.** Explain how something is like or different from something else. This helps people understand concepts you've presented.

Each presentation and each audience are unique. Because you can't predict what will happen when you begin a speech, you need to be prepared for just about any situation that may arise.

It's just like a winning football team that prepares a game plan for its opponent every week. The players never know exactly how the game will play out until they take the field, but they practice and come prepared. As a speaker, you need to do this too.

Some final tips for effectively presenting material include:

- As you begin each new topic, link it to the previous topic, show how it relates to the subject and present the benefits your audience will receive.

- For every piece of theory or concept you present, ask yourself, "So what?" That answer is the benefit or the "how-to" that people are so eager to get.

- Move quickly from descriptions of the problem to solutions to the problem.

- Use both male and female business examples.

- Design the flow of your ideas so that they move from simple to more complex and from general to specific. Plan to give an overview of each new topic, then fill in the details.

- Plan to communicate in small "bites." Present only one idea at a time.

- Avoid technical jargon; use familiar words and phrases.

- Summarize frequently. State and restate key ideas.

- Support each idea with concrete, specific examples. The most powerful examples come from your personal experience. Show results of actions. Use numbers.

- Plan to involve your audience through participation. You'll both be more comfortable.

- Never make ethnic, sexist, religious, political, or sexual references or use any foul language.

- Never refer to specific companies and then relate their wrong-doings.

- Never criticize yourself, the course material, the hotel, the brochure, the company, competitors or customers.

- Know your material cold.

## Summary

It's important to know what turns an audience on and what turns an audience off. In general, people like presenters to:

- Deal tactfully with disruptions.

- Be physically direct by moving toward them, making direct eye contact and increasing the volume of their voices.

- Be friendly.

They prefer presenters who avoid:

- Cleverness or clichés

- Sermonizing

- A "teachy" style

- Being too loud too early

- Constant hard driving

- Mismatching language and content

Good speakers always build rapport with their audiences. Doing an audience analysis or talking to the person who's setting up your presentation should help you determine how to best relate to people. If you can't do this, try these two techniques:

1. **Test the temperature.** Ask audience members some questions to learn more about them and to gauge their interest.

2. **Warm up the audience.** Many professional speakers use warm-up exercises to get things started on the right note.

Presenters and their audiences need each other. Without an audience, you have no one to listen to you. And, people usually come to listen to you because they need to do something or they need help with an issue affecting them either at home or work. Always put the needs and interests of your audience first.

One of the very best ways to build rapport with your audience is through humor. Here are six rules for adding humor to your presentations.

1. Use humor that fits your style.

2. Use humor that fits the occasion.

3. Use humor that fits the audience.

4. Use humor as a recess.

5. Make light of jokes that don't go well.

6. Use humor as a bridge or transition.

To cut down on interruptions, precall it at the beginning of your presentation to keep it from happening in the first place. Then if someone interrupts you, politely and diplomatically tell her you'll deal with it in the question-and-answer portion of your presentation.

Because members of your audience learn in three different ways, you have to use techniques that appeal to all three of them.

1. **Visual learners.** These people do best if you give them plenty of visual aids, pictures, text and graphs.

2. **Auditory learners.** These people do best if you tell them how to do something. Use voice variation.

3. **Sensory learners.** These people learn by touch and feel. Get them moving and doing.

# 5 PRESENTATION TACTICS FOR MEETINGS

After reading this chapter you will know:

- how to bring balance to each negotiating session

- 10 attributes that successful negotiators possess

- how to keep meetings on track and on time

In many instances, meeting presentations are nothing more than negotiation sessions. When you talk to a club's members about the benefits of donating money or materials, you're negotiating — you're trying to get them to volunteer. When you outline your plans for this year's PTA, you're negotiating — you're asking people to support your ideas. When asking for a raise, you want the boss to agree.

Successful and powerful negotiators don't go into a meeting with the sole intent of winning at all costs. They don't think or say, "I'm going to bury you today." Instead they approach each meeting with a win-win attitude, and they always seek a win-win solution. They want everyone who's participating to come away satisfied, as winners. In other words, they bring balance to each negotiation session. It is the same in a presentation.

You can do this too by answering these six questions as you prepare for any meeting.

1. **What basic beliefs are at stake for me?** Which issues are most important to me?

2. **What basic beliefs are at stake for them?** Which issues are most important to others in attendance?

3. **What's my payoff?** How much am I willing to compromise and still get what I want?

4. **What's their payoff?** How much will they be willing to compromise and still get what they want?

5. **Why is this difficult?** What hurdles do we face in reaching a compromise?

6. **How can I make this easier?** Look for ways to facilitate the negotiation process.

## Dos and Don'ts of Negotiating

To successfully negotiate during a meeting, follow these rules:

- **Do offer suggestions, don't disagree.** When you tell someone you disagree with him, it's the same as saying he's wrong. People don't like to be told they're wrong. Good negotiators instead say, "That's interesting" or "I understand, and there may be another way to look at this." This is such a subtle way to disagree that people may not realize what you're doing. Occasionally, someone may say something so outrageous that you shouldn't even bother trying to reason with them. Your efforts won't do any good.

- **Do present evidence, don't force positions on other people.** Good negotiators prepare by doing their homework; they come armed with facts and figures. They've got their act together. They never simply say, "Trust me, I know what I'm talking about."

- **Do rely on other resources, don't do everything yourself.** Don't be a "know-it-all" or the type of person who thinks, "Nobody can handle this but me." Others like it when you ask for their help. It makes them feel important and valued.

- **Do make it easy to save face, don't push people into a corner.**
  What happens when an animal is pushed into a corner? It usually
  attacks. People can be that way too. Don't allow people to feel like
  losers — that they're being forced to accept something. Find a way
  to make them feel positive about your negotiation session.

- **Do respect others' feelings, don't judge them.** Everyone has a
  right to his opinions, feelings and beliefs. Good negotiators accept
  and respect these, even when they don't agree with them.

Plan the opening of the negotiation in order to minimize conflict. Use a
leading question — one that the other party can answer positively. Use an
anecdote — a story that illustrates value to the other party. Another idea is to
use an endorsement from the other party.

Halt difficult situations by avoiding either/or positions and minimizing
us/them divisions. Rather than using the personal pronoun "you" in your
evaluations, try situational descriptions. Attack the problem, not the person.
Don't try to control feelings with arguments, persuasions or threats — use
facts and logic. Limit the number of decision-makers to those directly
involved with the conflict. A solution must have a quality of acceptance or it
will only be the source of further conflict.

Anger is an emotional response that is usually used as a defense
mechanism. When we are not getting what we want, when we feel frustrated,
thwarted or attacked, or when we feel righteously justified, we use anger to
defend our position. Anything you do that gets people emotionally involved
helps you bring the negotiation to a satisfactory conclusion.

Following is a list of 10 attributes that skillful negotiators possess and use on a regular basis. Put a check mark by the ones you've already mastered. For those you haven't, write down a couple of ways you'll work toward improving them.

1. Self-control

2. Social poise

3. Awareness of people, time and space

4. Tactfulness

5. Ability to be analytical

6. Decisiveness

7. Persuasiveness

8. Enthusiasm

9. Honesty/directness

10. Flexibility

# Reflections

## How to Be an Effective Meeting Leader

While people fear public speaking more than anything else, many business-people hate meetings more than anything else. They usually find them too long, too boring and generally unproductive. However, as a meeting leader, you can do several things to keep things on track and on time.

1. **Prearrange the seating.** In some cases you may want certain people to sit together or be separated. Try using name cards or simply asking people to take certain seats as they enter the meeting. You also can determine seating arrangements according to positions of power. The most powerful position is always at the head of the table. The second is located just to the right of that person, while the third most powerful seat is at the other end of the table. For a really fast meeting, remove the seats altogether.

2. **Establish external controls.** Of course, every meeting should have and follow an agenda. When possible, send these out in advance so participants know what will be discussed. If you're making a presentation during the meeting, you may want to appoint someone else to act as a moderator for the follow-up discussion. Other important roles during the meeting are those of note-taker and moderator. In most cases, you'll be too busy to do these yourself. Be sure that notes are compiled and sent out within a couple of days. Also be sure to keep the meeting moving and on schedule. You can help by not rambling during your presentation. If you have to, make a note that says, "No rambling!" in bold red letters. You also can ask a friend in the meeting to give you a signal — such as yawning or pulling on an ear — if you begin to ramble. E-mail is an excellent tool for providing agendas. Likewise, contact software can preannounce topics and roles.

3. **Foresee events when possible.** The same advice applies to meetings as well as to presentations. Anticipate possible problem areas and prepare for them in advance. Know who your negative people might be, what the hot topics are, then choose to precall, address problems head-on or simply ignore them.

4. **Delegate unknowns and monitor them.** Don't waste your time on things others can easily do instead. For instance, if you forget something in your office, ask one of your employees to get it for you. Stay focused on your intent.

5. **Look for "cheerleaders."** These people are on your side. They not only agree with you, they encourage you. They have "friendly eyes." Others may have "hostile eyes." They disagree with you, and they're just waiting for a chance to challenge you. Watch out because these people will drain your energy. You may begin to question yourself, "Did I say something to hurt his feelings? Is my material any good?" If you look for "friendly eyes," this will bring back your energy and recharge your presentation. Play to the cheerleaders, talk to them.

6. **Look for ways to crystallize issues.** Always try to strengthen or back up your material. Offer references and give examples of what you're talking about. Position all information in terms relevant to the audience.

7. **Don't be afraid to use the resources of your audience.** There may be times during meetings when you won't know the answer to a question. Perhaps it involves a project someone else is responsible for or a project you've delegated to one of your employees. If that's the case, respond like this: "Duane, you've been working on this for the past couple of months, how about helping Felicia with the answer?" However, if no one at the meeting knows the answer, just say, "I don't have that with me right now, but I'll get back to you later." Then, be sure to follow up. It's also okay to say, "I don't know." Some people are reluctant to do that because they think they'll appear foolish.

8. **Mark your notes.** Write little reminders to yourself in the margin of your notes. This includes things like "Don't ramble!" or "Slow down!" Also remember to number the pages of your notes. That way, if you drop them, you can quickly rearrange them and go on. Use color notations to trigger your memory.

9. **Don't panic, stay in control.** Here's more advice for dealing with interruptions. If someone challenges you during a meeting, remain cool. You'll lose respect and credibility if you say, "Who do you think you are? Get out of here!" Instead, respond with, "Tell me what you mean" or "Please explain your point" or "What you say is interesting. Let's talk after the meeting." If this tactic doesn't work, then say, "I'd like to discuss it now, too, but we've got other issues to tackle. We'll talk afterward." If the interrupter still persists, you may want to take a break for five minutes to deal with the situation. Remember: deep breaths!

10. **Triple-check all equipment.** Everything needs to be working properly — microphones, television monitors, tape players, computers or overhead projectors. You should know where all the light switches, outlets and the thermostat are located. Also have additional chairs and tables available in case you need them. Know the phone number of a local audiovisual company for bulbs, cords or rentals.

By having all of these logistics under control and taking time to prepare adequately, your meeting should run smoothly and efficiently. Those attending may even enjoy themselves.

## Materials Can Help Run a Meeting

High touch requires high tech for success with today's presentation needs. Consider adding these options:

- Audiotapes — short messages and easy to carry

- Blackboards — easy to use, easy to see

- Charts/graphs — show structure clearly, easy to use and transport, big impact, small cost, variety of types to choose from, can tailor to sophistication of audience

- Computers — possibilities for displays are endless, can prepare charts and graphs, easy to develop own presentations, easy last-minute adaptations, transport easy

- Diagrams — can be made in advance, several different types to use, can adapt to sophistication of audience

- Films — present slices of real life, good emotional appeal, popular, easy to use, show action

- Flip charts — can use several and draw in stages, can design in advance, can prepare whole presentation

- Handouts — inexpensive, prepared in advance, audience can use later, design can be bold and eye-catching

- Maps — can clarify discussion points

- Models — explain structure, function, design

- Overhead projectors — easily available, easy to use, predesigned, color allows emotional appeal, easy transport

- Photographs — can be visually stunning, provide details and descriptions, relatively inexpensive to produce

- Posters — can give much bang for the buck, inexpensive, easy to produce

- Slides — prepared by professionals, done from photos

- Videotapes — provide dramatic effective images, popular with audiences and speakers

**Simple computer design tips will increase your impact.** Use two bold fonts, one for titles (headings) and one for the main text. Have a maximum of three colors. Mix upper and lowercase letters. Don't use UPPERCASE, except where essential for emphasis. Your headings and subheadings should be consistent. Make the print large enough to be seen at a distance. All text should be well-spaced. And be sure you title all graphs and charts.

Media tools are created by combining media, including text, photographs/graphics, audio/music, videos, and animation. Multimedia becomes interactive when the user is asked to respond by means of exercises, prompts, questions, simulations and navigations. Interactive multimedia can produce better learning than traditional classroom instruction. Benefits include the multisensory stimuli (text, graphics, colors, audio, video) that create stronger, more lasting impressions. Instruction requires involvement and gives the learner a sense of control. The strength of individual instruction allows the learner to individualize the pace and sequence of his or her own learning. The programs are reusable for more in-depth learning or review. There is usually reduced learning time as compared to the same material with a traditional method of learning. The learning can correspond closely with on-the-job application. Programs are easily changed or upgraded.

Be careful, however. Multimedia works best when people are put in situations that are so realistic that they have a sense that something can and will happen to them. When training is learning-by-doing, multimedia adds reality. Multimedia gets people's attention and can persuade trainees. It works well when subject matter is concrete. Basic skills training and interpersonal skills like telephone sales are enhanced by multimedia. With soft-skills, like interpreting body language, it has lesser impact since instruction cannot teach a skill the same way in a similar situation over and over. Multimedia can lend itself to overdramatizing a presentation. Multimedia is a creative, demanding, multifaceted endeavor best done by teams. The final program is often very different than the beginning design. First-time producers have an extremely steep learning curve. The hardware platforms are often outmoded before program completion. Planning and attention to detail are the keys to success. There are no real shortcuts.

---

*"What hath God wrought?"*

— First words sent over the telegraph

*"Watson, come here. I need you."*

— First words spoken over the telephone

*"Are you receiving this?"*

— First words spoken through the Internet

And from the presenter: — *"I'm on but where do I go?"*

## Summary

Meeting presentations are nothing more than negotiation sessions. Successful and powerful negotiators approach each meeting with a win-win attitude, and they always seek a win-win solution for everyone involved by answering these six questions:

1. What basic beliefs are at stake for me?

2. What basic beliefs are at stake for them?

3. What's my payoff?

4. What's their payoff?

5. Why is this difficult?

6. How can I make this easier?

Here are some do's and don'ts of negotiation.

- Do offer suggestions, don't disagree.

- Do present evidence, don't force positions on other people.

- Do rely on other resources, don't do everything yourself.

- Do make it easy to save face, don't push people into a corner.

- Do respect others' feelings, don't judge them.

Skillful negotiators possess and use the following ten attributes on a regular basis.

1. **Self control.** Skillful presenters remain in control, regardless of what happens. They don't let internal or external forces ruin their presentations.

2. **Poise.** Not only is it important for a presenter to know presentation content, the trainer also must be perceived as someone who knows the subject about which he is speaking.

3. **Awareness of people, time, and place.** A good presenter will be cognizant not only of the people attending the presentation, but also of the most convenient time and place for them. A good presenter starts the presentation on time and ends on time.

4. **Tact.** Tasteless comments or jokes are bound to hurt individuals, as well as the presentation. Tactfulness is an important trait for all presenters. If in doubt, remain silent.

5. **Decisiveness.** Allowing participants to ask questions means that the presenter must be quick on his feet, able to process the question, facilitate group responses and provide "suggested" answers.

6. **Ability to be analytical.** The ability to be analytical, creative and knowledgeable requires constant study, openness and a love of learning.

7. **Persuasiveness.** A presenter is usually trying to get an audience to act or think in a specific way. In order to be successful, be persuasive.

8. **Enthusiasm.** If you can't exude true enthusiasm for the topic you are presenting, then you can't expect your audience to be enthusiastic either.

9. **Honesty and directness.** If your presentation deals with an unpopular or controversial subject, being honest and direct may be difficult. In the long run, honesty — no matter how painful — will pay off. These two attributes also affect your credibility.

10. **Flexibility.** Professional presenters should avoid being too rigid with timing issues. It is important to allow the audience's interaction to occur naturally, without presenter time constraints.

To keep your meeting on track and on time, keep these 10 rules in mind.

1. Prearrange the seating.

2. Establish external controls. Set an agenda and appoint someone else to act as a moderator and note-taker.

3. Anticipate possible problem areas and prepare for them in advance.

4. Delegate unknowns and monitor them.

5. Look for "cheerleaders," or people on your side.

6. Look for ways to crystallize issues.

7. Don't be afraid to use the resources of your audience.

8. Mark your notes as reminders.

9. Don't panic, stay in control.

10. Triple-check all equipment.

# 6 THE POWER OF VOICE CONTROL

After reading this chapter you will know:

- some exercises to strengthen and enhance your voice

- how to overcome annoying speech mannerisms

- how to add variety to your voice

Do you like the sound of your voice? Most people don't. In fact, many are startled and surprised the first time they hear themselves on a tape recorder or videotape.

Your voice actually tells a lot about you — how you feel about your subject, how you feel about your audience, how you feel about yourself, just how you feel in general. Also, many people tend to judge you by how you sound. It's unfortunate, but that's the way it is. So, the better you sound, the better you'll be perceived.

## Changing Your Voice

The good news is you can change your voice, including your volume, pitch and control. All it takes is hard work and persistence. Following are six things that will help you strengthen and enhance your voice.

1. **Watch what you drink while speaking.** Cold liquids, sugary sodas and caffeine contract your vocal cords, making it harder to talk.

Instead, keep some room-temperature water nearby. If your voice starts to go after you've been talking for a long time, ask yourself how many cans of soda or cups of coffee you've had. These always make it harder to keep your throat clear.

2. **Do face and voice exercises.** Start by stretching your neck, yawning and loosening up your voice and face each morning, especially when you have an early presentation to give. Just think how your voice sounds if you have to answer the phone in the middle of the night. Groggy, froggy and cracked — not very pleasant. Just as an athlete warms up before an event, so should you. Your event happens to be a presentation.

To loosen up your face, rub your jaw with both hands or just one hand if you're reading the newspaper or driving. (Try to ignore the strange stares from other drivers.) Also move your tongue around for a couple of minutes. If you think this is a little strange, remember that professional speakers, singers, actors and broadcasters all do exercises like these.

To prepare your voice, stand up very straight, take a deep breath and say "ah" in a normal speaking voice. Hold it for several seconds. Then take another deep breath and say "uh" in a very low register, again holding it for several seconds. If you repeat these exercises each day for a whole year, you'll notice your voice getting silkier and richer. If your voice is too high, concentrate on the lower "uh" sound. If your voice is too deep, concentrate on the upper "ah."

3. **Make your voice lower and slower.** In general, people whose voices are lower and who speak slower are seen as more authoritative and powerful. Those with high-pitched, fast voices are seen as flighty and frivolous.

4. **Pay attention to your tone of voice.** Your tone accounts for 38 percent of the message you send to other people. In other words, how you say something is almost as important as what you say. And remember, when you give a presentation your tone of voice is intensified.

5. **Rely on confidence and humility.** If you don't feel confident about the presentation you're about to give, your audience won't have confidence in you either. People will be able to hear the insecurity in your voice and see the apprehension in your body language. Also remember that nobody likes a cocky, arrogant speaker. Be proud, but humble. Try some affirmations before a speech, e.g., "I am a great speaker." Better yet, tape some affirmations of yourself to listen to as you go to the presentation.

6. **Practice, practice, practice.** Again, this is what the professionals do — and it's how they got where they are.

And how much should you practice? About 50 percent of the total time you've spent preparing your presentation. So, if it took you four hours to do research and to make a flow chart or notes, then you should practice about two hours.

Every chance you get — in the shower, in your car, in front of your family or even the dog — practice what you're going to say. You may want to tape-record or videotape your presentation so you can critique it later. Doing this also allows you to pick up on annoying habits, such as putting your hands in your pockets or constantly saying things like "okay," "well" or "know what I mean?"

## Speech Mannerisms

Speech mannerisms are habits — some good and some bad. The key is to keep the good ones and get rid of the bad ones. In either case, they're usually hard to break. First focus on eliminating the bad ones from your repertoire, especially the following:

- **"Uh-uh-uh."** Many speakers have an uncontrollable urge to always have a sound pouring from their mouths. For them, silence is unbearable. This mannerism becomes a "filler" before the next idea comes to them or even the next sentence. To overcome it, really concentrate on every word that comes out, and even try scripting a presentation so you'll know exactly what to say.

- **"You know?"** People use this for the same reason as the previous example. Avoid them both.

- **Weaving back and forth.** Moving around during a presentation is fine, but this is simply a symptom of nervousness. Besides being extremely distracting, it may cause your audience to get seasick or to worry that you'll trip over. Walking around as much as possible prior to your presentation is probably one of the best ways to stop weaving.

- **Licking your lips.** This is one of several annoying facial expressions, including grimacing, head jerking and excessive blinking. Break the habit by practicing your presentation in front of a mirror or by videotaping yourself.

- **Repeated and meaningless hand gestures.** While these usually add dramatic emphasis to your presentation, doing the same ones over and over become boring, anticipated and even unnatural. Again, practice in front of a mirror or on videotape.

- **Playing with things.** There's nothing more distracting than fiddling with things like eyeglasses, markers, keys, pocket change or note cards. Avoid picking up these things if they pose a problem for you.

Again, an excellent preparation technique is to videotape and audiotape yourself. Watch, listen and adapt.

If you're really having a hard time eliminating one of these mannerisms from your presentations, write reminders to yourself in your speech notes.

## Vocal Variety

This allows you to emphasize certain words so they "jump out" at your audience. Think of it as the vocal equivalent of an exclamation mark! Following are some ways to add variety to your voice.

- **Rate.** This is how fast you speak. Avoid talking too fast or too slow. Occasionally speeding up and slowing down will help you make a point or recapture people's attention.

- **Pitch.** You change your pitch by moving your register upward on an important word or syllable. For example, "You have a critical role to play in this project." Make sure to emphasize the words you want to really stand out. Practice key phrases over and over.

- **Volume.** Speak louder to emphasize important words or phrases. Speak more softly to make a point, comfort someone, involve someone in a discussion, or project gentle strength. However, if you're too soft-spoken too often, you may be labeled as too meek or mild.

- **Pause.** A short or extended pause can be an effective tool when you want to make a point. It gives your audience extra time to think about what you've just said. You may even want to script pauses into your presentation.

- **Lengthening words.** This technique can add drama. For example, "You don't need to do it that way."

Turn attention to your breathing. Try this exercise, which is best accomplished by lying on the floor; however, it may be done in a chair.

- Close your eyes and observe the rise and fall of natural, relaxed deep breathing. Do not make an effort; simply relax.

- Let lips fall apart and feel outgoing breath escape over the front of your mouth, making a small "fff" as it leaves your body. Wait for the breath to be replaced at the center of your body in its own time.

- Allow yourself to become aware of the natural breathing rhythm until it seems genuinely to have found its own pace and place deep inside.

Some additional exercises focus on sending an impulse for sound down to the center of the diaphragm.

- Let the breath turn to sound: Huh-huh.

- Repeat the sound on each outgoing breath in the rhythm of your natural breathing. Huh-huh (relax for breath to replace) huh-huh huh-huh.

- Alternate "huh-huh" and "fff" to see how close you can stay to the sensation of just breathing when you add sound. Make sure the "huh-huh" is a pure sound and the "fff" is a pure breath. It can help to think of sound as black, breath as white, and a breathy sound as gray. A clear thought will help to achieve a clear sound.

- Introduce thought of descending pitches to huh-huh huh-huh, beginning with a comfortable middle register note and dropping down note by note and ending with a low, loose sound that approaches a gargle. Do not push, but simply allow the voice to go as deeply down and inside the body as possible. If you feel a strain, move up a bit in pitch. Stay with your natural rhythm.

Slowly rise to a standing position, maintaining as much relaxation as possible.

As a presenter, your voice acts as your calling card in many ways. So, take care of it and use it to your advantage. Speak pleasantly and just loudly enough so that everyone in the audience can hear you. Breathe normally and enunciate each word so that everyone understands what you have to say.

Before each presentation, use this checklist to make sure your voice is as well prepared as your message.

1. Have I avoided cold liquids, sugary sodas and caffeine drinks?

2. Do I have a glass of room-temperature water sitting nearby?

3. Have I properly warmed up by stretching my neck, yawning and loosening up my voice and face?

4. Have I practiced making my voice lower and slower?

5. Am I aware of my tone of voice?

6. Have I worked on eliminating annoying speech and body-language mannerisms?

7. Am I confident, yet humble?

8. Have I practiced my presentation enough? (Remember, practice makes perfect.)

# Reflections

## Summary

Your voice actually tells a lot about you, and many people tend to judge you by how you sound. Fortunately, you can strengthen and enhance your voice by following these six techniques:

1.  Avoid cold liquids, sugary sodas and caffeine, and drink only room-temperature water.

2.  Do a variety of face and voice exercises.

3.  Make your voice lower and slower.

4.  Pay attention to your tone of voice.

5.  Rely on confidence and humility.

6.  Practice, practice, practice — about 50 percent of the total time you've spent preparing your presentation.

Try to eliminate any annoying speech mannerisms you might have. For instance, saying "uh-uh-uh" or "you know" is a way for some speakers to fill time before the next idea or sentence comes to them. To overcome this, try concentrating on every word, even to the point of scripting exactly what you want to say.

Become aware of other bad habits like weaving back and forth, licking your lips, making repetitive hand gestures and playing with objects. Practicing in front of a mirror or videotaping the presentation should help. Write notes to yourself about avoiding all of these bad habits.

Giving vocal variety to your presentations allows you to emphasize certain words so they "jump out" at your audience. You can do this by altering the rate, pitch and volume of your voice. Adding dramatic pauses and lengthening certain words are also effective.

# 7 DEALING WITH THE FEAR FACTOR

After reading this chapter you will know:

- the four levels of presenters and where you fit

- how to overcome the most common speaking fears

- how to use positive self-talk

After reading this handbook, are you still afraid of speaking at a meeting or on a stage? Hopefully, the tips and techniques outlined have helped you overcome at least some of your apprehension. However, the best way to conquer your fear is to actually give presentations every chance you get. Over time, you'll gain more and more confidence.

Each time you speak ask yourself: What's the worst thing that can happen? Then come up with a plan to deal with that. For instance, say your biggest concern is that no one will come to hear you. If only four or five people show up, make your presentation very informal. Have everyone, including yourself, sit in a circle. Still give your presentation, but open it up for questions and discussion throughout.

Here are some techniques to get over "the jitters":

- Stop making excuses.

- Learn the techniques of presentation.

- Thoroughly prepare for the presentation.

- Memorize the opening and the closing.

- Visualize success.

You can build confidence by planning actions.

- Use body language to appear relaxed.

    — Smile, glance at the audience.

- Start slowly, enunciate clearly.

    — Shoulders back, chin up, gradually speed up.

- Open with a genuine statement of recognition.

    — Connect with audience.

- Realize that you know more about the topic than your audience.

    — Position your information around the audience.

- Dress well, arrive early, plan for the unexpected.

For each of the following speaking engagements, think about the worst thing that could possibly happen to you. Devise a plan to handle it and any other situations that might arise.

1. Your boss has asked you to present your ideas for reorganizing your department and your job.

2. As a member of a local service group, you are asking for volunteers.

3. As a team leader, you need to outline your goals for the coming year.

## Four Levels of Presenters

According to National Seminars' research, there are four levels of presenters. Try to determine where you currently fit and how you'll get to the next level.

1. **The beginner.** About 20 to 30 percent of the North American population falls into this category. These people experience absolute terror at the very thought of addressing a group. In fact, they look for excuses not to do it.

2. **The basic speaker.** Almost half of North Americans — 40 to 50 percent — are basic speakers. While they don't experience terror, they do fear public speaking and would rather not do it at all. They never volunteer to speak and only do it when they absolutely have to.

3. **The advanced speaker.** Many North Americans — 15 to 20 percent — are advanced speakers, and they don't even know it! They suffer some anxiety, but they still regularly speak in front of people either at work — in sales or training positions — or as members of clubs and organizations.

4. **The pro.** These people, who make up 5 to 10 percent of the North American population, have no fear or anxiety about public speaking. Instead, they're excited and eager to do it. In this case, being a pro doesn't mean you're paid for speaking.

## Overcoming Common Fears

All speakers, no matter how experienced or inexperienced, have some of the same fears. Following is a list of the most common fears and how you can work to overcome them.

- **Forgetting.** Everybody forgets now and then, even the pros. When they lose their train of thought, they often digress by saying something like, "Are there any questions?" While the audience thinks about that, the speaker has time to walk back to his notes and find his place. Actually, pauses like this can build up some drama in your presentation. Likewise, you can ask the audience where you were. Being human can add humor and make audiences even closer to you.

- **Looking foolish or being embarrassed.** Once in a while you're going to do something embarrassing. It's inevitable. What really matters isn't what you do, but how you recover. For instance, if you fall down while presenting, just get up, dust yourself off and say "Watch that step back there. It's a killer." You're sure to get a chuckle from the audience. Too often, presenters take themselves much too seriously.

- **A shaky voice.** This happens when you're visibly nervous and not getting enough oxygen to your brain. The best remedy is to take some deep breaths. If this doesn't work, try tightening your rear — rechannel that energy somewhere else. Another possibility is to imagine your audience without any clothing. That may calm your nerves or cause you to burst out laughing.

- **Sweaty palms.** You can't realistically cure sweaty hands, but you can bring along a handkerchief and wipe your hands periodically throughout your presentation.

- **Dry mouth.** Sipping room-temperature water should take care of this.

Each person fears something. For many of us, it just happens to be public speaking. Writer Ernest Hemingway probably put it best when he said: "He who conquers his fear with dignity has courage as well."

Even professional speakers get butterflies a few minutes before they begin a presentation. The difference is that they've learned to channel that nervous energy into something positive and dynamic. You can learn to do that too.

## Self-Esteem and Self-Talk

The number one factor that determines your individual success or failure is self-esteem — how you feel about you. The higher your self-esteem, the higher your chances for success.

At the same time, all of us talk to ourselves — as much as 70 percent of the time during any given day. Self-talk can be both positive and negative. Unfortunately, a lot of self-talk weighs in on the negative side with the should-haves, would-haves and could-haves of our lives. These chip away at our self-esteem, fuel our fears and send inaccurate messages that blur reality.

For example, you may tell yourself, "There's no way I can stand up in front of my peers and give the quarterly sales report. I'm afraid I'll make a fool of myself." In some cases, negative self-talk like this becomes a self-fulfilling prophesy. If you believe you'll fail, then you will.

However, you can turn these negative messages into positive affirmations. You can program yourself for success through conscious, positive self-talk. Although it may seem awkward at first, it is one of the easiest and fastest ways to change your behavior and overcome your fears. Positive self-talk focuses on possibilities, positive outcomes and "can do" thinking.

Here's an example of positive self-talk: "I'm really looking forward to giving the quarterly sales report at the staff meeting. After all, the boss wouldn't have selected me if he didn't think I could do it. With preparation and practice, I know I can do it too."

Following are four positive self-talk steps you can use to help overcome your fear of public speaking.

1. **Tell yourself what you're afraid of.** "I'm afraid of giving the quarterly sales report at the staff meeting."

2. **Explain to yourself why you have this fear.** "I'm afraid I'll make a fool of myself."

3. **Rationalize why this shouldn't be a fear.** "These people are my co-workers, and many of them are friends. I talk to them individually every day. Why should talking to them together as a group be any different?"

4. **Close with a positive statement about yourself and your ability to make the presentation.** "I'm a quick study, and I know these sales figures inside and out. With preparation and practice, I believe I can give a good presentation."

   Make an audiotape of yourself. Listen to your presentation over and over, instead of memorizing. You will gain confidence hearing your own words.

   Also, make a tape of affirmations. "I am a great speaker." "I am really interesting." "I am smart." "People love hearing me." Again, hearing affirmations about you in your own voice locks into the brain.

Take care of yourself and your self-confidence will grow.

*Don'ts*

- Before speaking or performing, avoid eating heavy meals and eliminate dairy products, chocolate, nutty, syrupy, and sweet foods — all of which produce phlegm.

- Avoid caffeine and alcohol, which strip the body of moisture.

- Do not smoke.

- If you have a cold or sore throat, don't cough loudly and avoid numbing throat sprays.

*Do's*

- Exercise regularly to keep the body toned and to increase abdominal strength in particular.

- Keep regular sleeping hours. Fatigue stresses the voice.

- Eat lightly before speaking or performing.

- Be sure the voice is properly hydrated. Drink plenty of water.

- Observe good oral hygiene.

- If you have no time for a vocal warm-up, use a vocal "chew." Move your mouth as if chewing, repeating the word "YUM" and concentrating on the chewing motion, rather than the sound produced.

- If you have a cough or sore throat, the following remedies may be of use:

  — Use a vocal "tap" instead of a cough to get rid of phlegm.

  — Drink warm liquids (honey and lemon may be added in moderation).

  — Gargle with salt water (1/4 tsp. salt to glass of warm water).

  — Suck on lemon drops or mild cough drops.

Think of a speaking opportunity you turned down or almost turned down because of your fears. Work through each of these positive self-talk steps to overcome your fears and get ready for your next opportunity.

1. Tell yourself what you're afraid of.

2. Explain to yourself why you have this fear.

3. Rationalize why this shouldn't be a fear.

4. Close with a positive statement about yourself and your ability to make the presentation.

Reflections

Some tips to reduce apprehension include:

- Focus on a single object for thirty seconds while breathing deeply.

- Plain old deep, slow breathing is a great control mechanism.

- Crumble a napkin or a piece of paper into the palm of your hand and squeeze as hard as you can for five seconds.

- Rub your hands together rapidly and focus on the build-up of heat and energy.

- Clench both fists tightly and punch downward.

There's no easy solution or magic potion that will make you a fearless, confident and competent speaker overnight. It takes work, and it all starts with P & P — preparation and practice.

For those of you who are beginners or basic speakers, just do it. The next time your boss chooses you to give the quarterly sales report or you're asked to lead a PTA meeting, jump at the chance. The only person standing in your way is you.

## Summary

Before each presentation, ask yourself: What's the worst thing that can happen? Devise a plan to deal with it and any other situations that might arise.

National Seminars' research indicates there are four levels of presenters:

1. The beginner, who experiences absolute terror at the very thought of addressing a group.

2. The basic speaker, who doesn't experience terror, but who would rather not do it at all.

3. The advanced speaker, who suffers some anxiety, but still does it.

4. The pro, who has no fear or anxiety and who's excited and eager to do it.

Following is a list of the most common fears and how to overcome them.

- Forgetting. Say something like, "Are there any questions?" and then walk back to your notes and find your place.

- Looking foolish or being embarrassed. It doesn't really matter what you do, it's how you recover.

- A shaky voice. Take some deep breaths.

- Sweaty palms. Bring along a handkerchief so you can wipe your hands periodically.

- Dry mouth. Sip room-temperature water.

You also can overcome your fears and program yourself for success through conscious, positive self-talk. Follow these four steps:

1. Tell yourself what you're afraid of.

2. Explain to yourself why you have this fear.

3. Rationalize why this shouldn't be a fear.

4. Close with a positive statement about yourself and your ability to make the presentation.

The secrets of a memorable presentation have been discussed throughout this handbook. Reinvent your concepts; introduce and discuss familiar ideas in a personal way. Continually focus on benefits to the audience and give the audience clear guidance by building in concrete applications.

Provide visual information. While always considering visual aids, develop ways to show information visually through vivid experience or mental pictures to create mental images.

Conquer the fears of speaking through preparation, practice and confidence. Add continually to your experience by presenting frequently.

Use funny anecdotes and examples from personal experience. Find areas where humor is appropriate and pull from actual happenings.

Create analogies, similes and metaphors. Be creative in how information is presented and made real.

Consult experts, watch and listen to others present. Research how and what others do and learn the art of synthesis.

Listen to yourself. Audiotape or videotape yourself, noting strengths and points of need.

Save, study, and build a library. Acquire stories, quotes, analogies and organize them by topic and type of supporting material.

Build your formula for speaking success. Consider:

- Likability — connect with the audience as soon as possible.

- Audience needs — know specifically what they are and where/how you will cover each promise.

- Define the theme — a one-line thread through which all information is connected.

- Transitions — clearly scripted to lead into each topic, page and out of each topic, page.

- Well-organized conclusion — containing transition, review, a humor piece, an appeal, link to emotions, challenge or direction.

- Involved, active introduction — identifying yourself, need for topic, humor, audience connection, overview, precall of any negative possibility.

- Involvement — activities, interactions, questions, tests.

- Humor — built in.

- Timing — set up so that appropriate time is allocated for all elements.

- Content — specific to topic, to demographics of audience and per time available.

- Effective communication skills — overviews, summaries, concise presentations.

- Constant focus on and with audience — listening and adapting to audience, allowing participation.

- Physical presence and position — moving deliberately into and around audience in specific places, for specific reasons.

- Verbal communication pace — faster than slow, more aligned with visual learner.

## Presentation Evaluation Form

Use this form each time you make a presentation. If you look at it before you speak, it will serve as a reminder of all the things you should do. If you look at it after you speak, it will help you evaluate how well you did and where you need to improve.

Think of it as a tool that will allow you to grow as a presenter. You also can use it to evaluate other speakers. Simply circle the plus sign if you (or another speaker) did a good job with each element listed. Circle the minus sign if improvement is needed.

### OPENING

| | | |
|---|---|---|
| Greets participants before opening | + | - |
| Opens with a strong statement | + | - |
| Encourages meeting neighbors (communication) | + | - |
| Sets up the day (logistics, breaks, etc.) | + | - |
| Introduces materials to be used | + | - |
| Uses name tags | + | - |
| Introduces self (establishes credibility) | + | - |

### FIRST IMPRESSIONS

| | | |
|---|---|---|
| Image | + | - |
| Enthusiasm | + | - |
| Credibility | + | - |
| Confidence | + | - |
| Poise | + | - |

| | + | - |
|---|---|---|
| Approachability | + | - |
| Immediate participation | + | - |

## VOICE

| | + | - |
|---|---|---|
| Vocal variety (to impact audience) | + | - |
| Tone quality | + | - |
| Volume | + | - |
| Rate of speech | + | - |
| Articulation | + | - |
| Handling of microphone | + | - |

## GROUP INTERACTION

| | + | - |
|---|---|---|
| Questions to the audience/show of hands | + | - |
| Questions to specific people/call by name | + | - |
| Repeating of questions to the audience | + | - |
| Handling of audience responses | + | - |
| Asking audience to take notes or write down | + | - |
| Group exercises/audience participation | + | - |
| Giving specific "how to's" | + | - |
| Movement throughout audience | + | - |
| Control of theory/lecture | + | - |
| Relevance of examples/stories | + | - |

## PRESENTATION SKILLS

| | + | - |
|---|---|---|
| Gestures | + | - |
| Eye contact | + | - |
| Smiles (use appropriately) | + | - |
| Purposeful movement | + | - |
| Lack of distracting mannerisms | + | - |
| Natural use of hands and arms | + | - |
| Facial expressions | + | - |
| Pauses for impact | + | - |
| Humor and use of one-liners | + | - |
| Playfulness | + | - |
| Setting up materials/using transitions | + | - |
| Summarizing benefits frequently | + | - |
| Repeating key points | + | - |
| Use of sequential materials | + | - |
| Energy | + | - |
| Pacing | + | - |

## VISUAL AIDS

| | + | - |
|---|---|---|
| Use of transparencies/slides/projectors | + | - |
| Use of props/demonstrations | + | - |
| Use of books and articles as references | + | - |

## CONTENT

| | | |
|---|---|---|
| Sincere message | + | - |
| Promises kept | + | - |
| Match between program and outline/materials | + | - |
| Use of quotes, examples and illustrations | + | - |
| Use of stories | + | - |
| Personal ownership of materials | + | - |
| Continuity of message (thread) | + | - |
| Encouragement of feedback | + | - |
| Creation of word pictures | + | - |
| Clear instructions | + | - |
| Proceeding in a logical sequence | + | - |
| Emotional appeal | + | - |
| Making a point without being redundant | + | - |
| Establishing human values | + | - |
| Handling of questions from the audience | + | - |

## CLOSING

| | | |
|---|---|---|
| Summarizing | + | - |
| Confidence | + | - |
| Maintaining enthusiasm | + | - |
| Delivering what was promised | + | - |

Closing with a challenge/conviction/emotion       +       -

Complimenting audience                            +       -

Establishing audience rapport/likability          +       -

# INDEX

**D**

Deductive
   Model   39-40, 46
   Presentation   39-40, 46

**E**

Elements of presentation   3, 6-7
Extrovert   21-23, 26, 28

**F**

Fear   iii, 4, 69, 85, 88-91, 93-95, 97, 99, 101, 108

**G**

Gray-Zone speakers   3, 19, 24, 28

**H**

Humor   3, 15, 34, 41-42, 49, 55-58, 63, 89, 95-96, 100

**I**

Inductive
   Model   39-40, 47
   Presentation   40, 47
Interruptions   3, 59, 63, 71
Introduction   iii, 6, 12, 14, 30, 32-34, 36, 41, 46, 96
Introvert   21-23, 26, 28

**J**

Judger   21-24, 28

# Notes

# Notes

# Notes

# Notes

# Notes

# Notes

# Buy any 3, get 1 FREE!

**Get a 60-Minute Training Series™ Handbook FREE ($14.95 value)\*** when you buy any three. See back of order form for full selection of titles.

These are helpful how-to books for you, your employees and co-workers. Add to your library. Use for new-employee training, brown-bag seminars, promotion gifts and more. Choose from many popular titles on a variety of lifestyle, communication, productivity and leadership topics. Exclusively from National Press Publications.

## DESKTOP HANDBOOK ORDER FORM

Ordering is easy:

1.  Complete both sides of this Order Form, detach, and mail, fax or phone your order to:

    **Mail:**      National Press Publications
    P.O. Box 419107
    Kansas City, MO 64141-6107

    **Fax:**         1-913-432-0824
    **Phone:**     1-800-258-7248
    **Internet:**  www.natsem.com

2.  Please print:

    Name_____ Position/Title _____

    Company/Organization_____

    Address_____City _____

    State/Province_____ZIP/Postal Code _____

    Telephone ( ____ )_____ Fax ( ____ ) _____

    Your e-mail: _____

3.  Easy payment:

    ❑   Enclosed is my check or money order for $_____ (total from back).
        Please make payable to National Press Publications.

    Please charge to:
    ❑   MasterCard      ❑   VISA      ❑   American Express

    Credit Card No. _____ Exp. Date_____

    Signature_____

• • • • • • • • • • • • • • • • • • • • • • • • • • • • • • • • • •

### MORE WAYS TO SAVE:

SAVE 33%!!! BUY 20-50 COPIES of any title ... pay just $9.95 each ($11.25 Canadian).

SAVE 40%!!! BUY 51 COPIES OR MORE of any title ... pay just $8.95 each ($10.25 Canadian).

\* $20.00 in Canada

# 60-MINUTE TRAINING SERIES™ HANDBOOKS

| TITLE | RETAIL PRICE | QTY | TOTAL |
|---|---|---|---|
| 8 Steps for Highly Effective Negotiations   #424 | $14.95 | | |
| Assertiveness   #4422 | $14.95 | | |
| Balancing Career and Family   #4152 | $14.95 | | |
| Common Ground   #4122 | $14.95 | | |
| Delegate for Results   #4592 | $14.95 | | |
| The Essentials of Business Writing   #4310 | $14.95 | | |
| Everyday Parenting Solutions   #4862 | $14.95 | | |
| Exceptional Customer Service   #4882 | $14.95 | | |
| Fear & Anger: Slay the Dragons …   #4302 | $14.95 | | |
| Fundamentals of Planning   #4301 | $14.95 | | |
| Getting Things Done   #4112 | $14.95 | | |
| How to Coach an Effective Team   #4308 | $14.95 | | |
| How to De-Junk Your Life   #4306 | $14.95 | | |
| How to Handle Conflict and Confrontation   #4952 | $14.95 | | |
| How to Manage Your Boss   #493 | $14.95 | | |
| How to Supervise People   #4102 | $14.95 | | |
| How to Work With People   #4032 | $14.95 | | |
| Inspire & Motivate: Performance Reviews   #4232 | $14.95 | | |
| Listen Up: Hear What's Really Being Said   #4172 | $14.95 | | |
| Motivation and Goal-Setting   #4962 | $14.95 | | |
| A New Attitude   #4432 | $14.95 | | |
| The New Dynamic Comm. Skills for Women   #4309 | $14.95 | | |
| The Polished Professional   #4262 | $14.95 | | |
| The Power of Innovative Thinking   #428 | $14.95 | | |
| The Power of Self-Managed Teams   #4222 | $14.95 | | |
| Powerful Communication Skills   #4132 | $14.95 | | |
| Present With Confidence   #4612 | $14.95 | | |
| The Secret to Developing Peak Performers   #4692 | $14.95 | | |
| Self-Esteem: The Power to Be Your Best   #4642 | $14.95 | | |
| Shortcuts to Organized Files & Records   #4307 | $14.95 | | |
| The Stress Management Handbook   #4842 | $14.95 | | |
| Supreme Teams: How to Make Teams Work   #4303 | $14.95 | | |
| Thriving on Change   #4212 | $14.95 | | |
| Women and Leadership   #4632 | $14.95 | | |

| **Sales Tax** | | | |
|---|---|---|---|
| All purchases subject to state and local sales tax.<br>Questions?<br>Call<br>**1-800-258-7248** | **Subtotal** | | $ |
| | **Add 7% Sales Tax**<br>*(Or add appropriate state and local tax)* | | $ |
| | **Shipping and Handling**<br>*($3 one item; 50¢ each additional item)* | | $ |
| | **TOTAL** | | $ |